Angling Days

Jack Bevan

'The pleasantest angling is to see the fish
Cut with her golden oars the silver stream'

William Shakespeare – Much Ado About Nothing

Published by Sigma Leisure – an imprint of
Sigma Press, 1 South Oak Lane, Wilmslow, Cheshire SK9 6AR, England.

British Library Cataloguing in Publication Data
A CIP record for this book is available from the British Library.

ISBN: 1-85058-732-9

Typesetting and Design by: Sigma Press, Wilmslow, Cheshire.

Cover Design: Design House

Illustrations: Christine Isherwood

Printed by: MFP Design & Print

For my brother Ken

"And what should I do in Illyria?
My brother he is in Elysium"

Also by Jack Bevan

Verse

Dragon's Teeth. *Guild Press, 1956*

Brief Candles. *Outposts, 1962*

My Sad Pharoahs. *Routledge and Kegan Paul, 1968*

Translations

Selected poems: Salvatore Quasimodo. *Penguin, 1965*

Debt and Credit: Salvatore Quasimodo. *Anvil, 1973*

Complete Poems: Salvatore Quasimodo. *Anvil, 1983*

Journey with my Friend (Viaggio con l'Amico): Francesco Berti. *George Mann Books, 1999*

War Memoir

Through the Donkey's Ears. *George Mann Books, 1997*

Contents

1

Lying Fallow

The close season is, for all trout fishermen, a time for savouring the past and anticipating the future. For me, the season has just ended. It is mid-October. Any normal person, glutted with indulgence in his favourite pastime, would bow out gracefully, lay aside his toys and say to himself, 'Lusisti satis', enough is enough. Now I know well enough as I lay aside my tackle that it has by no means seen the last of me until the opening day on the first of April. In about a month's time, I would guess, I shall find some excuse for going to the place where my tackle hibernates and taking it out again, lock stock and barrel (if that is a close enough image) for a complete inspection. The ritual goes something like this. I take out the contents of my fishing bag and empty them on the floor. I inspect each item with the doting fondness of a mother for her only-begotten son, in whom she is well pleased. I notice the wild mint I gathered and stuffed in the bottom one hot day by the river. It has dwindled now to a handful of dried dust, but such aromatic dust! That day comes back to me excitingly as I potter.

There is the large wallet of casts, 'floating' on one side, and 'wet' on the other – I notice the label on one of them and recall the musty shop in Ross-on-Wye where I bought them two or three (heavens! six) seasons ago. I re-arrange them unnecessarily, grateful for the service their brethren have given, some on my reels still. Next, I take out the bottle of fly flotant, and imagine I am about to drop one of my favourite flies, safely secured to its light leader, gently into it. I remember the chap who told me at the riverside that he always treated his flies the night before. I firmly resolve to continue to pursue the luscious vice of dipping my flies as and when I tie them on. I like whipping them about to dry them before crouching to present them to my quarry. Every angler has his own preferences, and let nothing woo him from them. What a man likes to do, he will do well. Guiltily, I take out two more half-filled bottles of flotant, and wonder why I thought I had only one. I know in my innermost heart that one rainy day last winter my footsteps led me involuntarily to my favourite fishing tackle shop, and before I knew what I was doing I was thumbing through a trayful of flies, muttering to the smiling 'keeper' that I needed some March Browns. Then, as he hovered like a trout in prime condition behind the counter, I added that I also needed a bottle of fly flotant. I told myself that I might run out of my present supply. But I knew that he knew only too well why I was there. It was winter. The town was wet and full of soulless people buying soulless things. The river was only a distant vision and I wanted to keep it alive, and the way to do it was to get inside the tackle shop as smartly and as unobtrusively as possible. Having bought my items, I found myself going upstairs into the sanctum sanctorum, a timeless place where the fishing season was never over. I browsed among fishing hats, deerstalkers, peaked caps, and tore myself away, recalling the six or seven assorted types of headgear I already possessed, purchased on similar occasions. I dallied over waders, regretting that mine were still perfectly adapted to my needs. Fishing waistcoats, fishing jackets, waterproof gear with large pockets and tempting arrays of brass zips held me musing, until I remembered my Barbour, light, waterproofed, zipped and press-studded, with concertina pockets, and I drifted reluctantly away. Reels held me for a while, but I have never been a reel fetishist, so I pressed on, led as if by a hypnotist, to the rods. It was after about fifteen minutes that the voice of the 'keeper', who had moved. from his lie behind the counter downstairs, broke in on my reflections. He murmured something about 'a beautiful little tool for the brook' and handed me a cane wand, a mere six feet in length, so delicate, so beautiful, that he must have heard the sharp intake of my breath as I took it. I weighed it, caressed it, plied it, while his gaze rested on it with a reverence equal to my own. I drifted out of the shop with the March Browns, the supernumerary bottle of fly flotant, and the cane wand to add to my collection. That rod made the time of waiting for the season to open seem endless. I used to feel like that as Christmas approached, thinking, as my brother did, of the all-silver pedal car in Hill's Bazaar which we had coveted for months. We never acquired it. We were a large family, and it was beyond our means. Perhaps that is why I felt such guilty joy in my new cane brook rod. In any case, the event explains how I came to have such a rich supply of fly flotant.

My scissors come out next, attached to a loop of old flyline for going round my neck. They are small, with plier tips, very useful for removing a recalcitrant fly from a well-hooked trout, or a well-hooked jacket sleeve. I wind its fastening round it, and think of the many times I have been saved from frantic burrowing in pockets or bag by its friendly dangling round my neck.

Next come the reels. I note with satisfaction the smooth joining of two or three feet of heavy nylon to the end of each line, so that when I knot on a cast which may not be tapered, the stiffish nylon attachment helps it to loop out straight. For the moment I do no more. At the back of my mind, I am aware that there are months to go before I dare let myself really go in preparation for the first sortie, fully cocked, trimmed and limbered, to the river. I lay them on one side. My eye now falls on the safety pin which for years has been clipped (or one like it) to the strap of my bag. It is another delay-saver and panic-avoider. Long ago, as the only riser of the day wallowed a few yards upstream, and tying on a different fly became a Sisyphean task, I made it a rule to always have scissors and safety pin to hand. So often the scramble to get the point of the leader through the blocked eye of a fly and my failure to achieve this has led to a frantic search for a sharp point to free it. And even then, with the fly tied on, the search for the missing scissors to trim off the quarter-inch of nylon from the tie has been so nerve-racking and of such long duration that by the time I have started casting, the trout has decided to dine elsewhere. Or in my eagerness to make up for lost time I have botched the first throw, and have banged the fly down on the water so hard that the fish has disappeared upstream with a large wake to tell his wife and family that they are drilling for oil.

Then, out comes a tiny plastic pillbox of line-sink, which never loses its lid in the bag. Next, I cautiously take out a similar box, full of assorted split shot, the lid of which, for some reason, invariably comes off at the bottom of the bag. I promise myself that I will make that close season visit to the tackle shop again this year and buy one of those boxes fitted with dispensers. Meanwhile, I scoop from the bottom of the bag as many shot as I can find, and drop them in the box. A small bottle of glycerine now appears, with which, on occasion, I dunk wet flies to make them sink without reliance on the leader to sink them. It has been with me for years. I am very fond of that flat, neat little bottle, and think with contempt of the days of my spent novitiate when my bag was weighed down by large flagons of such commodities as this. In those days I was too headstrong to plan my campaigns in the fallow season. In my fervour to be off, I even forgot such vital items, or failed to calculate how many thousands of years it would take me to use up half a pint of glycerine in dunking wet flies.

A small flashlight now comes out and I test it. How often, when others are overtaken by dusk and are unable to change their fly for the sedge, which is being eaten noisily by the late diners, have I profited by its presence in the bag. How often, like them, have I cursed the darkness as I held up a fly to the sky in years gone by. One of the most heart-rending sights on the river as the angler returns with full bag to the stile where his car is parked, is that of a lone fellow angler a few yards away in the gloaming, both hands held up before his eyes. As he attempts to tie on a fly, faint sounds of anguish and hurt are coming from him. You sigh and proffer the torch, which he seizes with a glad cry, and you watch with satisfaction a few moments later as he grapples in the semi-darkness to get the thing at the end of his U-bent rod to the net.

Appropriately, I find next in my bag the eight-inch piece of heavy dowelling which serves as a 'priest' for the last rites. I have never possessed the made-for-the-purpose gadget. In my experience, the articles most often lost by the riverside are these. It may be because they are brought out at the most exciting (or at the culmination of the most thrilling) moments of the whole exercise. They are used, by the wise, on the trout as it lies in the net. They are laid aside in the grass while the fish is removed, the fly detached and placed away from the net. The fish is then placed in a plastic bag, which has to be searched for in the fishing bag, and stowed away. The net must then be folded, the bag replaced on the shoulder and the net hung on the strap. After this, the loose line on the rod must be wound in, the fly examined and hooked near the butt. The angler then moves off in search of the next riser, his mind and heart full, leaving the priest in the grass.

Another neat, round box now appears, containing line flotant, or, more appropriately in these days, leader flotant. I inspect it, and place it with the others. Various oddments follow. A small whisky flask, a tiny reel of fine copper wire, and other savouries.

Now comes the big moment, which I have saved to the last: the flies and nymphs. There are two metal fly boxes and a wallet. I open the first, the slimmer of the two metal boxes. It contains mayflies, nymphs, daddy-long-legs and other imitations whose size warrants a box of their own. The other box has a metal leaf, hinged in the centre. The left half contains dry flies, the right half wet flies. The wallet, which I far prefer to the boxes, also has a dividing leaf. On one side, lined in foam rubber, lie the nymphs, grubs and pupae, and on the other side the lake flies and lures. I gloat for a few minutes, again aware that in a month or two I shall rearrange them all, and, as if the fallow season should put them all out of my head, I shall make a key to their names on a postcard. I replace them all in the bag, my hands lingering on the leather wallet as I slip it into the side pouch. As I do so, I recall the look of misery on the face of an angler whose countenance, as it peered at me through the long reeds where I was casting, betokened almost the final horror. He had lost his fly box. What can one do, or say, in the presence of grief and desolation? Of course I laid aside my tools, murmured consoling words, and searched the banks and reeds for a quarter of a mile with him. But he was a stricken man, like a researcher who has lost five years of notes. I saw in his face the desperation of the miser who has lost his treasure. That scene remains etched in my memory. After that it became a ritual with me to keep my flies in a snug side pocket of my fishing bag, safely strapped down. If ever I transfer them to the pocket of my fishing jacket, the flap is always closed with a snap of press-studs. All anglers have their private rituals. This is one of mine, even though, I shamelessly confess, I do not tie my own flies. I love the idea of having this as a close season hobby, and can well imagine that all notable fly anglers would curl the lip at a tyro who could not, in half an hour, produce a few of the right articles for the next day's fishing. But I know myself. I know the irritation I would feel at my clumsiness. What would be the devising of a tasty artefact to another, would be fiddling to me. So I envy the man who makes his own flies, admit his superiority, but remain strictly an absentee from the fly-tying class, skulking off to the tackle shop for my entomological software, and gratefully accepting a home-made fly from a fellow angler when offered one. In return, I always produce my box and wallet and ask (insist) that he takes his pick. I invariably find there is something there he will fancy.

Looking at the bag as I muse, I realise that the loss of a fly box is the penultimate, but not the final horror. The worst is yet to come. Let no seasoned angler tell me that in all his career by river or lake he has never stepped on his rod, or had it stepped on by a friend. My waders crushed the butt end of my rod by the Kentish Stour many years ago. I was well aware that to lay a rod on the ground is to court disaster. Mine was propped against a low bush while I unbuckled a fish I had just netted. But in the ritual of dispatching, unhooking and bagging the trout, I forgot all else and turning, trod on and sprung my rod. Ironically, had I laid it flat on the ground the damage would have been less. I will draw a veil over the gnashing and lamentation, and merely point the moral for beginners. It will happen to you, but once it has, it will never happen again.

Looking at gear, of course, includes waders, fishing jackets, hats, eye-shields, polarised glasses that tilt to any angle (the best invention ever) and anything the individual taste deems to be a desideratum. I once knew a man who kept a copy of Shakespeare's sonnets in his fishing bag, and would rather have set off without his landing net than leave them behind. Another insisted on keeping a length of light rope, with a heavy iron nut tied to one end. He was a careless caster, elderly, and bad on his feet. It was a pleasure to see him, when snagged in the lower branches of a tree, hobble to his bag, extract the rope, and holding one end, hurl the iron nut into the foliage again and again, until it had looped the offending branch. Then, with a snarl of rage and delight, he would heave at both ends until the lower twigs were within his grasp, and the fly could be extracted. This same ingenious gentleman, bowed down with years though he was, would never, if snagged in the riverbed, say goodbye to his fly and cast before putting the iron nut to a further proof of his ingenuity and determination. He would untie it from the rope, chuntering to himself, tie it with a tiny loop of string round his line, then pay it out gently and painstakingly, easing his rod up and down until he felt it to be in the right proximity to his fly. He would then give his rod one or two twitches. On the occasion when I witnessed this extraordinary performance, the fly came away clean as a whistle, and he proceeded, puffing and blowing, to enumerate its merits. He had tied it himself, which perhaps accounts for his addiction to it.

I now conclude my gloating by taking down my fishing jacket. It is very dear to me. We have all tried out many sorts and varieties, and found them wanting until we know we have found the one that serves all our occasions. In my case this is a light Barbour, and I cherish it. I must here gainsay my earlier remarks about keeping some of the more mouth-watering chores until the close season is at least half over. Yesterday I proofed my fishing jacket with an odorous confection in a tin bought for the purpose. I first warmed the jacket until it lost its stiff brown paper quality and hung like a rag in my hands. Then for a blissful hour I plied over every inch and seam until it gleamed like a sunbather at Portofino. After a night in a

warm cylinder cupboard it is now proofed and I can recount its
charms. It is light, unlined, and looks like an oilskin but isn't. It
reaches over the top of my waders. It is shaped and charmingly
smocked in functional key places. It has a hood, which I double into
a half-sphere to stand up behind my head when necessary. It has a
gathered cord at the waist and hood. It is fastened by a strong,
well-designed zip, with a generous overlap for four brass
press-studs. There are press-studs also at the wrists for cold days
and a sailor-suit flap behind the hood, also held down by
press-studs. The pockets are large and deep, with flaps designed so
that they bend over the tops of the pockets so that no water can enter. The flaps are also equipped with brass press-studs. It is the answer to the fly angler's prayer. Clad in waders and this, he can never
be wet. On a cold day in the early days of the season, with
polo-necked sweater and warm jacket, he can put it on and be
armed against the coldest wind. On those beguiling spring days
when the sun shines warm, he can leave it open and remain cool, for
it is a featherweight. In summer it can lie at the bottom of his fishing
bag, rolled tight, occupying no space at all, ready for any rainstorm
that is foolish enough to challenge him. It is a garment for all seasons, unequalled, the apple of my eye. I would (dare I say it? I must,
for no angler can lie when talking of his obsession) yes, I would
rather lose my best rod than lose this paragon of jackets.

After this, the waders, held upright by cord attached to a hook in
the cupboard, are of no great interest. You can see them in any
tackle shop. Enough to say that waders should be as lightweight as
possible. During the fishing season, when all my gear is kept in the
boot of my car, so that wherever I go I am ready for the fray, there is
also present a pair of very light wellingtons. So often on a summer's
day, when deep grass is still wet, wellingtons are all that is required
to keep one dry from the knees down. In most of the places where I
fish nowadays it is not necessary to enter the water. Waders then
become a protection merely against bad weather, and in summer
are hot encumbrances. It is true that there are occasions when I
curse the lack of them and with their help could reach a riser by
edging a yard or so into the river. It is a question of priorities.
Wader-less you cannot reach some fish. Wader-less and cool you
can walk further and meet up with others within reach. But enough

of waders. Steer clear of the man who, because he is wearing them, seems determined to wade. Once, in the Alps of Piedmont, I saw some hens in a pasture at about eight thousand feet suddenly disappear with loud squawking and clucking. A goatherd saw my surprise and pointed at the sky. Half a mile away, and high up, so that it was only a tiny speck, circled *l'aquila*, the eagle. They would not venture out again for hours he told me. Something has programmed the alpine hen's eye retina to register an eagle or a falcon when it is only a speck in the sky though it may not see an Englishman at thirty yards! So it is with trout. Bowline waves, disturbed mud, all send out their signals loud and clear. So the wader is to be given a wide detour.

Let us now leave gear and tackle. I am glutted for the moment. There are, after all, other solaces in the fallow period for the pining angler. I belong to an association with several miles of river and several lakes at its disposal. There is much work that can be done, and must be, in the close season. Weed has to be taken out of the lakes, jetties and boats have to be painted and repaired. The boathouse and its gear must be seen to. Lost anchor weights must be replaced, paddles checked. On the river, undergrowth and brushwood have to be cut back. On suitable days, a nip in the air and a flood of wintry sun bringing out the russets, browns and duns of woods and spinneys, I repair to the river. With no one frequenting its banks in the close season, I have it all to myself. I wander to my favourite places and do the things that with a rod in my hand there was never time to do. Now I carry a long pair of secateurs and a rake. I seek out these offending branches, those overgrown thorns that have so unerringly caught my fly on the backcast, even waiting for the last false cast in order to madden me most. They fall prey to my seeking blades, and I gather them in piles with the rake and deposit them out of harm's way. The rushes that hid an angler completely have now withered and fallen obligingly. I note a low branch that on another occasion I shall take a cross-saw to, and some half-submerged roots I shall coax out with a rope and hook. But there will be a limit to my cathartic clippings. Without trees, high boughs, and the occasional tunnelled reach, the river would lose its charm and the delight of those large fish that survive the season to tantalise the angler, who on a hot summer's day, has to crouch, wade, curse, cast no more than head high to put a fly over them. Of course, the main

purpose of these occasional forays is clear enough; I can't stay away
from the river for more than a week or two. By going there with the
alibi of one-man working party around me like a label, I can drink it
all in, relive past angling excursions, and plot future ones. Can I
believe it was here one summer evening in the half darkness that I
had that thrilling take with a sedge? I can see now the place where it
swallowed my fly. Then, with the reeds and rushes eight feet high, I
could not even see the river, narrowed to no more than a brook by its
growth on either bank. I only *heard* the rise, and had to raise my rod
high above my head in order to cast the yard or two upstream where
I guessed the fish was feeding. I remember my surprise at not getting
snagged in the dark on the backcast, and my even greater surprise at
the instant take. Netting him through the dense growth between the
water and me was a problem. But the brown trout of a pound and a
half was real enough when I took it out of my bag in the light of the
car headlamps ten minutes later.

Now all is visible. The river has had all her mysteries laid bare as
I stand at the brink and meditate. It seems like another world. The
heat of the dusk, the biting midges, the sounds of the rising trout are
gone. But they will be there again, infallibly, in due season. "Yea on
the shores of darkness there is light." Sometimes, when (to quote
the same poet) "the melancholy fit shall fall" it is to the river, in its
widowhood, that I again return, the sickle a mere token in my hand.
I walk for miles beside its turnings and twistings, not seeing, but
hearing it. Unlike the lakes, which would turn their blank eyes
upward, the river talks to me. It is busy going somewhere. It has no
time to be morbid, but·chatters to me in a very practical sort of way
about how it almost flooded last week, and what a nasty, brownish
complexion it has now. It never moralises as I do, and I am thankful
for that.

The annual general meeting is another close season treat, but of
that I shall speak elsewhere. For the moment, let me describe that
greatest of all comforts in the fallow season, a fishing companion. I
have had, in the past, all sorts of companions in my fishing, but only
a few fishing companions. There was a colleague, years ago in the
Dales, who was as fanatical as I was. But circumstances limited the
times we could go fishing together, and after one season he left the
snug market town where we lived to take up another post. Rare
returns to my birthplace in the north and renewal of my brother's

friendship made us both return to childhood. An hour after arriving he would be showing me rods and reels. My mind would return to the world of ponds, or 'pits' as we knew them then, and the mystery that invested them. Each pit had its monster of the deep – carp, or tench or roach – and in our minds they had grown even larger since our inept boyhood efforts to capture them. The mention in a local record of six six-pound tench taken in the mere towards the end of the last century was still sharp in our memory. Within another hour we would have our gear ready, and would spend the evening planning excitedly. It was always a four o'clock start, with bacon placed hot between thick slices of buttered bread as our haversack rations to be consumed by ten o'clock, to the accompaniment of hot tea from thermos flasks. A visit down the garden to the compost heap ensured full bait tins, and off we would go. The mesmeric effect of watching a red-tipped float through the ripples hour after hour still haunts me. The quick bobbing, or the sideways slow submersion was the fulfilment of youthful yearnings long gestated. With my brother beside me, telepathically in tune with me, it was hardly necessary to talk. Yet talk we did, mostly of fishing. And as soon as one expedition was over, and the tackle was being stowed, we would be busy excitedly planning the next. My brother had that essential quality of a fishing companion ... unlimited enthusiasm, equal to my own. There was no need to coax or lure him with recounted tasters. He was there ahead of me always and I bless his memory for it.

Another fishing friend, this time of days on the Kentish Stour, was a man then twice my age. More of him elsewhere. It was he who introduced me to the finer points of dry fly-fishing on the river that flowed at the bottom of my garden. True, he was of a different breed, and of a temperament which would have precluded any likelihood of companionship other than at the river. But he was a strong influence, and I still remember all his gestures and habits. He had retired at the age of forty, and had spent the last forty-three years in the pursuit of trout. What he did not know was not worth knowing in the matter of trout, their habits and preferences. For all I know he may be fishing still.

For the last two seasons my friend the family doctor has occasionally accompanied me on one of his rare and precious days off. He arrives at the R.V. suitably attired and, in the early days of the season, with a good supply of Bovril. As we drive to the river the talk is copious, and always of fishing. As his practice covers a large area of countryside, he is acquainted with a goodly number of farmers, and over the years he has fished lakes and ponds and brooks by the dozen. There is hardly a turn of the road or a bridge or a glimpse of water that does not elicit a fishing story. Above all, he is an enthusiast, and therefore a good fishing companion. A year or two ago I had a colleague for a brief period who fished with me, a Welshman with whom I had hardly more than a nodding acquaintance until we discovered our common weakness, the flaw that set us apart from other men. From then on he seemed to acquire several more dimensions. I saw him in a quite different light. He became for me a more complete, more fully rounded human being. Once embarked on fishing lore, he could not stop. And he was ever ready to embark. At the river there was never a fear that, when we split up after a hasty snack at the pub, each for our different beats, the time for the evening rendezvous at the stile need be taken too literally. And on meeting again we would agree to fish on beyond dusk without hesitation. Inured as I have been to the shortcomings of lesser fishing companions (not mentioned) in the past, to whom enough was enough after an hour or two, these stalwarts stand out. No need for the special plea ("There's one rising under the footbridge, a good 'un.") with them. They carried their own motivations with them, and had no need of mine.

But what of the fallow season, vis-à-vis angling companions? This season, an ex-colleague, a hitherto non-angling friend, otherwise kindred spirit, has been at my side many times as I fished the river and lakes. Gradually, by stealth, tasters, a few intriguing captures, and occasionally by letting him 'have a go' I have induced in him an unmistakable desire to dally next season with a fly and wand of his own. Early in this process, with subtlety and cunning with which I surprised even myself, I gave him an old rod with a spare top and a reversible butt with a spinning section for the winter foray after pike. After a few more jaunts, and a fishing book or two to devour between whiles, I could see the gradual 'take'. For a while I played him. A week or two ago I landed him at the AGM and he is now in the bag. He devours the literature, has introduced me to some, and being a scholar, has found it easy to master the basics on paper. In retrospect, I realise that what had deterred him at first was his conviction that, charming though it all was, he would be incapable of mastering the business of casting. Handling the rod at the riverside and lakeside has satisfied him that he can do it. He has already bought some tackle, acquired another rod, and like me is all set for the next season.

Here comes the relevance of all this to the fallow season. Imagine a friend with common interests and a common professional background who is also 'willing, wanting and waiting' for fishing talk at the fireside. I shall be to him what I always sought in my apprenticeship and never quite found; one who will answer every question and help to shorten the period before he stands on his own two feet. When the season begins I shall no longer shadow him with advice. He will make his own decisions, make his own mistakes, and enjoy the thrill of capturing his first fish. He can hardly wait; nor can I.

With such a companion, another palliative to the pains of waiting for the spring renewal is the possibility of a little pike spinning. I love spinning for pike. The next time he calls I shall take out my pike tackle and the result will be, if I am not mistaken, a trip to a nearby lake where pike and perch are to be had. I shall tell him of the afternoon downstream from Fordwich when I fished the old lakes that border the river and in the light of a frosty sun brought out and returned fourteen pike, the smallest nearly ten pounds (the largest not much more!) before darkness chilled me away. From the river that flows a few yards away I have had sea trout in June, though almost all my fly-fishing on the Stour was done in the city water upstream from Canterbury. Here in winter there was also the bonus of spinning out the many jacks from the trout water. And all for the cost of a rod licence!

This I shall tell him, adding Izaak Walton's account of the 'Fordidge' trout, which I cannot resist quoting now:

"There is also in Kent, near to Canterbury, a trout (called there a Fordidge trout), a trout that bears the name of the town where it is usually caught, that is accounted the rarest of fish; many of them near the bigness of a salmon, but known by their different colour; and in their best season they cut very white; and none of these has been known to be caught with an angle, unless it were one that was caught by Sir George Hastings (an excellent angler and now with

God); and he hath told me, he thought that trout bit not for hunger but wantonness ..."

I remember seeing in the local museum some vast, prognathous fish, which I then thought too big for trout. Were these 'Fordidge' trout? Such will be our winter talk and speculation, the close season stuff of angling companionship.

Pike spinning in winter is a great boon, especially when it does not require an expedition to be reached. There is a piece of water beyond a village near where I live which offers this boon. Within minutes of leaving, the eager pike spinner can be walking along the lakeside, spinning as slow and as deep as he dare. True, fallen trees in one part, propped deep in the lake bed, account for many a pike trace and spoon. Knowledge of the water after a visit or two helps him to avoid familiar snagging places, and it is not uncommon, on days of frost when the pike are taking, to be kept busy with bent rod. My spinning rod is the one I have had since my first serious spinning days began. The top section is of a pale, milky, plastic material, whippy, like stiff rubber, and it fulfils all the functions I require of it. It is the length of a short brook rod and is the handiest tool for its purpose that I have come across. The walking-stick-length spinning rods on the market may serve on unencumbered water, but where there are reeds and undergrowth at the water's edge I like a rod with a reasonable tip that I can manipulate and control. This reminds me that before I dive for the second time this close season into my fly-fishing tackle I must sort out my pike gear and make it ready for a sudden sortie. After fly-fishing, there is something about steel traces ... Spinning for trout in the Chislet marshes once I remember being annoyed and puzzled at finding my spoon gone on three successive casts until I realised that the jacks were out on patrol. That was the beginning of my initiation into the fascinating pursuit of Mr Luce. Now, I would guess that I must have five or six pike traces made up among my pike tackle. I think I have even included one or two minnow flights for spinning a small dead bait when spoons and wobblers fail. Yes, I feel that very soon I shall be off for the pike. Writing about it has whetted my appetite, so tomorrow or the day after ...

That is the greatest delight of the fallow season. The water still calls, though the trout rods are down and in their cases. As I talk with friends, or read, or write, or think about it I am reliving it, recreating past thrills and lying fallow for fresh ones. And meanwhile, delights of another kind of fishing offer themselves to my all too ready imagination. I am not one of those who fish on for the dazzling quarry until Christmas in the lakes and pools where this is nowadays possible, though I can understand their desire to do so. Let me confess it; I regret but welcome the five months in which I go without, like a Lenten faster. It sharpens the appetite, and gives me time to be thankful for my hunger.

One of the fly angler's legitimate solaces in the close season is the possibility of a little grayling fishing. I remember a day of ice and frost with intervals of warm sun when I rode on a motorbike with my brother over the winding road through Embsay and Eastby, up over Eastby Brow, down to Bolton Abbey, then along and across the Wharfe by Barden Tower to Appletreewick. Here the grayling gave us magnificent sport, and we returned, skidding and slipping in the winter dusk, 'huge and mighty forms' around us, to thaw out by the fire. Such days bring us into contact with what Wordsworth describes as 'unknown modes of being', and provide us with images that 'flash upon that inward eye' long after.

To recreate an experience is to relive it. That is the point of the fallow season to me. Looking at my tackle, talking with friends, visiting water I have fished in the season, and above all, writing about it, crystallises the past and helps to shape the future. Memories of those past encounters are not mere flies caught in amber. They are moving films. Of course, other things are happening. Life is for no one a mere fishing trip. But these are the pleasant background images that colour and tinge all the rest with the rosy cast that redeems the spirit. Without the presence, or the living memory of running water, trees, sedges, the interplay of light on leaves and grasses, something in me dies. My inner being withers. My youthful companions were dryads, naiads and oreads. Real? Imagined? I cannot say. But I still long for them.

2

The Artist Going to Work

There is a picture by Van Gogh from which I take my title. It evokes a summer morning, light dazzling in the foreground; in the background the distant town like a faint blue mirage, and in the middle ground is the small figure of the artist walking to his beat, a sunhat on his head, a short shadow dancing along with him at his feet. It expresses the joy of whoever sallies forth with hope in his heart. Angling has always been for me a return to a primal state of being. It is accompanied by a sort of rapture, in which I both lose and find myself. A light, springy wand in my hand, the right reel and line, an early June day with the mayfly on the river and the water trembling around my waders, that is eternity in an hour (or eight hours, it will be pointed out when I return at dusk!). I cease to be whatever I am supposed to be by virtue of my profession and way of life. When I go fishing I revert, as the science fiction writers put it. I become both hunter and hunted.

I belong to a club which has several long beats, uninterrupted except by a village, of a little sandy river which flows through rich farmland. It is bordered by pastures, spinneys and arable land, crossed at intervals by footbridges, narrowed to a brook in places by low sandstone cliffs. Six miles 'meandering with a mazy motion' it threads its way, the home of voles, waterhens and wildfowl. When it decides to colour, it stays coloured for days. Among the brown trout there are dace of considerable size, and one or two chub. But the trout is king here and there are gravelly shallows ideal for spawning. Such is the happy situation I spent all my early years aspiring to. I often had to search for my fishing, journey long miles for it, fight to find time for it. Now here I am, with miles of pheasant-thronged river at my elbow, and no one to say me nay. I am my own master, and can lay aside my work at the drop of a hat. And when the rushes and reeds have grown so tall that the favourite spring runs and riffles are inaccessible (for this is a mere nymphet

of a stream, almost under the legal limits for the official title of river)
I can change focus and turn my attention to a group of trout lakes a
few miles beyond. Nestling in a sequestered arcadia, they would
have made Theocritus sit up and take notice. With all this I feel
richer than Croesus. With such metaphorical fat to feed on in the
lean months of the close season, when the last day of March is out I
am still, figuratively speaking, fatter than the fattest of the trout that
will fall to my depredations in June's plenitude.

So here I am, full as Pharaoh's kin with my plenty, arriving at my
river tryst in typical mood. Now that we have been properly introduced, my angler friend, and because we are kith, which is sometimes closer than kin, you may travel with me in these harmless
revealings of my reverted self, and perhaps recognise your own.

3

May Morning on the River

It is a sunny morning in late May. I am off to the river. The air is full of 'cool warmths' and voices carry. It is all green and gold as I drive off. No need to check that I have the right tools for the job. From the first of April until the middle of October I keep all my tackle, including waders, wellingtons and Polaroid glasses in the boot of my car, so that wherever I go, should the opportunity arise, I am fully armed. I turn near the village, the scene of this morning's operations, and halt at a box hidden behind a creeper on the wall of a cottage. There, lifting the flap, I find books for both beats of the river and sign in, noting with suppressed delight that no one else is on the river. Entries for the last few days indicate that the fish have been moving, and fish of a pound to a pound and a half have been taken. Over the cattle grid, up a long drive, round the shoulder of a hill about half a mile, then down a steep track to a stile where we park. No one is there. I step out and breathe the delicious air. To right and left the pastures lie, and the river winds two hundred yards away, the focus of it all. I open the car boot, trying to be casual, but I am full of suppressed excitement and stumble back against the car as I pull on my waders and pass my belt through them. Next I put up the rod, select a reel with a light, floating line and pass the leader through the rings, laying the rod horizontal, the reel handle facing upwards. I postpone attaching the fly until I see what is happening down at the river. I sling my bag, attach the Polaroids with their tilting hinges, dangle a pair of small scissors with plier tips round my neck, slip a bottle of fly flotant, and a box of line grease in my pocket, and lastly clip the landing net to a ring sewn on the strap of my bag behind my left shoulder. I snap down the boot lid, climb the stile, and walk down through the pasture to the river. A warning here. If you are feeling gloomy, even on such a day as this, don't take your gloom fishing with you. The silence and beauty will only mock you and heighten your misery. Angling is for the mind at peace, however temporarily.

This is the moment, perhaps the best in the whole day, with everything still to happen, the water yet untouched, a cuckoo calling, the riverside still a mystery, alive with insects, a waterhen dipping and splashing unaware. Now comes the moment for honesty. I do not meander upstream, looking for rising fish. That will come later. At present I intend to explore the possibilities of the twenty or thirty yards of river on my right, downstream. It is arcaded over with trees, and ends with a glide under a bridge to an old mill pool. It is hardly more than a foot deep in the centre, where I can see the sun lighting the sandy bottom in a strong beam of light through the trees. The water shelves deeper under each bank, where reed beds

not yet up through the water make a good lie for trout. In this place earlier in the season I have often contacted fish, and once took three, almost in successive casts, from their lies under the bank, each about six feet downstream from the previous one.

This little reach can only be fished wet, though I once, last season, offered a floater to a rising fish by walking upstream, casting down until I had positioned the fly in the slow current, and walking quickly down to the riser, crouching double. By overtaking my fly, I was able to wait and see it pass over the right place. A yard below where it had been rising it took my fly with an easy swirl. Hallowed by such events, this reach seems ever full of possibilities. The bridge and the trees make casting upstream almost impossible. As there is nothing showing, I open my fly tin and select a Butcher, attaching it to a sinking cast. I dunk the fly in glycerine, apply line sink to the cast, and am ready. I think to myself that if I keep it moving in the slow current, down and across, it is unlikely to snag. By this time I am so eager that I am clumsy as I crouch double and manoeuvre myself into the edge of the river. I try to create as little ripple as possible as I find a position where my backcast has just a chance of missing the branches of the tree under which I stand.

My first false casts are messy, as always in my experience. The leader is not yet wet enough and tends to go out in coils. I trail it for trial through the water, then give it an extra couple of yards, shoot the line, and manage to land it (if that is not a contradiction in terms) under the opposite bank. I mend the line so that the belly on the leader straightens with the current and drift it slowly, letting the fly get well down, to the centre. Hopeless to try to get it to drift beyond the centre and bring it back along the nearside bank, because the current is too slow, and I am standing upstream on a bulge of bank, in line with the middle where my fly will end its crossing. Just as it arrives at the centre, where the sun is spotlighting the bottom, a slow swirl, almost on the surface, and I am tightening slack line, the rod bending, and the trout diving into the deeper water from which it has been lured. Two or three more attempts in different directions, a few lusty oarings away and round, and I can see him at last. Suddenly it is all over. He hangs passive in the water; I get his head up and glide him into the net. Happily, I note he hasn't run downstream, so there is still some water to explore between where he took me and the bridge. I extract the fly from the side of his mouth and lay him in the grass. Fourteen inches, I measure on my bag strap; one and a half pounds, I guess. Later he turns out to be just one and a quarter. In a small river this is a typical miscalculation. Absorption scales everything up. Every reach is enlarged by the imagination, every corner becomes a bay, every startled pheasant a jaguar. It is surprising, as I look up and around, to realise how relative is the matter of size, and to see the Amazon reduced to its proper dimensions. But the day is still young and has begun well.

My temperament is such that, having demonstrated to myself that I can choose the right place and method, offer the right fly in the right place, and move it so that it takes (or, more exactly, is taken by) a trout, the rest of the day will be a success whether I take others or not. An angler needs something to boost his morale, and this is it. In his heart he knows that in this place, on this bright morning, the fish would have probably taken any fly he cared to offer. And if he had put it down with a splash, towed it at twice the speed, the result might have been the same, though no angler would risk taking a chance against his knowledge and experience. So I smile with self-satisfaction and consider the next ploy. Our association rules that after taking two fish from a beat, an angler must desist from fishing that beat. No matter. The beat beyond the village is charming, and there are miles of it there waiting, if I take another here and have to move.

I decide that while I have a few more yards to try downstream towards the bridge, I might just as well do so as change to a floating leader and fly and look for rising fish upstream. So I edge downstream for two or three yards, weighing up the elements of visibility and room for backcast because of a large tree under which I have to stand. In this position I have to cast over my left shoulder, hold the rod above the reel to shorten it, and hope to shoot enough line to compensate. A trial or two casting short, then down it goes, four yards lower down the opposite bank than before. Immediately, the fly is taken, before it has sunk an inch. I tighten up, stripping back line, the rod doubling as I make contact. I can see the trout crossing that amber-brown spot in the centre. Suddenly he runs towards me. For a second or two the line is slack, though I stumble back and away in an effort to tighten. Then he is away and free downstream, his route marked by a V-line in the water. I bring the fly in, wind up, and sigh. No matter, I have had two thrilling encounters in this tiny stretch and have exploited its possibilities for the moment. Anyway, it means that I can continue fishing the beat.

Time now to change the leader, fill a pipe and begin a leisurely perambulation upstream in search of risers. I carry out the first of these appetising tasks sitting on the bank in the sun. When it comes to which fly, I ponder. I haven't seen any rising fish. Why not a nymph? If there are risers of the type I have heard called 'oncers', no doubt there will be more fish feeding on the nymph than on the surface or in the surface film. This way I shall not be waiting, but flicking my wand every yard of the way upstream. Time enough to change to dry fly when the nymph fails or when I spot a regular riser. Thus I meditate, complete the tying on and move up to a likely reach, twenty yards away and about thirty yards in length, beset with perils of overhanging grasses, ahead, a small hawthorn, and a tall bank behind me where every few casts I must inevitably be caught up. I take this as an invariable concomitant to fishing a small river and not going for only the safe places. I neither curse nor frown. This is not that kind of day. Elsewhere in these pages I shall have to reveal the manic side of my nature, my belief in demonic possession on the part of inanimate objects. I shall describe (though not repeat) the kind of language that pours cathartically from my lips on windy days when my best-laid schemes go not to order but 'agley'.

The face of creation smiles today, and I am at one with it. Here and now, at least, all is for the best in the best possible of worlds. I throw the nymph easily upstream. There is no breeze. The leader straightens nicely, the nymph plops in and sinks, and I chaperone it back to me with the current, letting it sink, bringing it to the surface, then letting it sink again. Despite the floating leader the weighted nymph takes itself down among the reedbeds. A sudden pause in the leader's movement indicates a take, but I am too slow on the strike. I proceed as before, enjoying the act of casting and watching. I approach a right-angled bend at the end of this little run and throw the nymph at the middle. As soon as it touches it is seized, and the silvery glitter in the sun indicates a dace. I net it, measure, eleven and a half inches, and place it back in the water. Even as I bend to clean my hands in the river there are dace rising in a shoal just ahead. So I climb up the bank, under the wire, and decide to walk on past bends, pools and twists, to a place upstream by a footbridge where the water runs more swiftly, rippling and shallow.

Here there is no wire to keep out the cattle, and no tall vegetation. Twenty yards ahead the river creams round a bend and narrows to a sluice hardly more than a couple of yards wide, then opens out again. There, in the slack at the side of the sluice, and six inches from the bank, is a regular riser, culling the provender washed back in the eddy. No use casting up over the sluice. The only chance is to throw the fly out and twitch the line at the moment of entry so that it falls with a little slack. The two or three seconds before the fly is dragged away by the force of the runnel may be enough. I am full of confidence. This is a situation within my experience, years of fishing a tumbling brook in Shropshire having taught me the hard way. There is nothing I don't know about small eddies, glides, sumps under little falls, and the way, even on a windless day, the air currents from the rushing water can take a well-cast fly yards out of its course before it falls. Even a small overhanging dock leaf can catch the fly. I have learnt to keep as much line and leader as possible in the air and out of the water, and to tweak, lift and slacken almost in one movement. I know that a feeding fish in these circumstances has its attention fixed on a few inches of fast-moving current, and is not easily disturbed. Even a hooked leaf a foot from its nose goes unnoticed, and a sharp, upward tweak to free the fly will see you in business at the next cast.

This trout is surfacing every twenty seconds. It 'has its eye in'. It is not idly surveying a wide window and catching sight of a yard of fine nylon. It is sighting an area of about six to ten inches square. It is lying in a tiny area of slack water, and its nose remains lined in the direction from which the food is coming so regularly. It is taking small things that fly past in the surface film, and when the stimulus of these is felt, the response is instant. There is no time for this fish, in this position, to consider, inspect, follow a foot downstream and take. Even here, with quick decisions to be made, a trout can take and reject in an instant. And here, with so many takes every minute, I feel the odds are with me. In my mind I am already notifying the registrar of births, marriages and deaths and making the funeral arrangements. Nevertheless, from habit, I crouch low in the water, and to avoid letting the rod be seen, I shorten it by holding it above the reel and dangle slack in the water to avoid false casting. One cast away from the spot to adjust the length, then over it goes, right on the nose. The trout grabs, just too late as the nymph is snatched away by the current. I pause. Still rising. I replace the nymph with a small Greenwell, dry, which I dunk in the water so that it will sit in the surface film. I cast again. The same thing happens. Not enough slack. The trout moves too late. I cast again, twitching the line at the moment of entry, and the fly falls perfectly. The foot of slack nooses a tiny root. The trout makes a magnificent lunge, takes the fly. I pause, tighten, and the root holds. There is a commotion, then peace. The trout, anchored to six inches of three-pound nylon, has known what to do. The funeral is off, and when I have also broken myself from the root I surprise myself by feeling no ill will. My offered fly was taken. The rest was just bad luck. So I content myself with a baleful look at the tiny root protruding from the bank an inch above the water and light a cigarette.

While I select another small Greenwell, my favourite all-purpose fly, and tie it on, the sounds of the river take over. Their trebles trickle into my thoughts. The cuckoo's call, 'at once far off and near' is like the flies on the water, part of the beautiful here and now, unique, never to be repeated. Last year's ephemera are gone, however much the creatures of this vernal moment resemble them. Everything flows but comes again, in the same form. Nature, unlike the human heart, is constant in her eternal renewing. Persephone leaves us each year, but 'with the flowers she comes again' and her face shows no sign of a year's ageing in the underworld. Only in the human heart is there decay without renewal, farewell without return. There, indeed, 'the rose's scent is bitterness to him that loved the rose'. I look around and see the very heart of truth and beauty, and hear in the water's voice the vow, never yet broken in human memory, that she will meet me here next year, renewed, unchanged... and even wearing my favourite dress.

But à nos moutons, as my French master used to say when we had led him into a digression from the main theme. Before I proceed up the river I owe the reader a brief confession as to my credentials.

In the matter of angling I am an amateur. I have won no accolades for casting, taken no specimen monsters from river or lake, have rarely fished the chalk streams and am far too ham-fisted to dress a fly or even make a good job of splicing a line. Worse (and forgive me if I shock you) when I tie on a fly I pass the leader through the eye, knot the end, clip the remnant beyond the knot, then make a simple overhand and pull it tight. In mitigation, I must say that I have never lost a fly because of the knot, and can do the job as quick as lightning. There are other, worse things you must know. In the matter of tackle I have always, until very recently, had shoddy equipment...and loved it. Second-hand rods have been my lot since I began as a boy. You must remember that angling was not then a popular sport. Bookshops, libraries, radio and television had not yet flooded the market. In those days a rod, a reel and a few flies had to serve for a long time. I am still amazed when beardless striplings show me sets of expensive rods, fly boxes containing hundreds of flies, reels of every kind, spinners, plugs wobblers, minnows and spoons by the dozen and whole ranges of line; floating, fast sink, slow sink, sink tip, and shooting head. When I ask how long they have been at it, they grin like seasoned campaigners and remind me that we exchanged greetings on the river as far back as last season! Nowadays, the cult of equipment has priority, and the palate is ruined before the appetite has developed. The purist will remind me that the better the equipment, the more likely the job will be well done. I am sceptical. To triumph over a sprung top section of a split cane rod, or to contend with the wrong reel-line-rod weight ratio is no bad part of an apprenticeship. To come to good equipment late is one of the joys and rewards of experience. Once, in the Serchio valley during the Italian campaign, long starved of fishing, I got a 'tiffy' to contrive a crude spinner. With this, a large bobbin of twine and a radio aerial, I proceeded to the river twenty yards away during a 'Stand Easy' of the guns, and was into a good fish in minutes, to the cheers of the whole battery. Snow was deep on the ground, and though the plump padre remarked that it was out of season, he ate his mouthful with the rest.

Obviously, I am not a perfectionist. I am too enthralled with the aura of fishing to spoil it with pernickety considerations. I am also afraid of spoiling myself with indulgence. I feel that if I have the perfect tackle for every occasion I shall offend the gods, walk on the red carpet, and retribution will follow. For me it is better to wish for a thing and not to have it, than to gluttonise. What is life if there are no more treats in store? When I bought a superb carbon fibre rod to celebrate a certain occasion last season, it was like at last having that silver motor car in Hill's Bazaar, which at Christmas my brother and I prayed for and never acquired. Only those who have managed in their childhood with Number 01 Meccano sets can ever deserve the Number 7, displayed in the shop windows of memory. We never got the silver motor car, nor the air gun, nor an even respectable Meccano set. But I dare say that if some fairy now produced that gleaming car, we would squeeze into it, fondle the red steering wheel, and poop the horn in disbelief at our good fortune. Instead, let us say, I have the rod, and can enjoy that in a way the beardless stripling just mentioned would be incapable of. 'You have played enough,' his spirit will say to him too soon. Mine still smiles and says, 'Play on.'

Enough has been said, I hope, to convince the reader in these meanderings, digressions and divagations (so like this river) that I do not speak as the master (heaven forfend) but as an enthusiastic devotee. I have nothing to teach you, but much to tell. And in the telling there may be something to be learnt. But I waste time. Downstream, in a stretch which I detoured, is a line of chestnuts spreading high over the river. I am hoping, in the fullness of their flowering, to try under the shelving bank at their roots where last year on such a day as this I had two minutes of dalliance with a lone riser of gordion shape and dazzling hue. Once brought to my net, I returned it to the river as a libation to the gods. Such stippled magnificence of rose moles was too persuasive. I walk downstream.

That silvery light of earlier spring, the sheen on beech boles and the close-packed wood growth of the thronged spinneys have departed, as remote as the photograph of a child of four now shaping to adolescence. The chestnuts as we arrive are an emerald canopy lining the bank, their pink spikes of blossom somehow suggesting kinship with the finned creatures beneath them. I pause, my attention usually so exclusively concentrated on the surface, distracted by all this glory. Beyond, the river, bending and twisting past the mill wheel through a great meadow and into spinneys where it loses itself in unfishable secrecy, gives form and meaning to this 'sweet, especial rural scene'. In the late morning it seems all laid out to the eye of heaven alone, and I an intruder. The silence, and the absence of human voices, contribute to the feeling of being both hunter and hunted already noted.

As I gaze I become aware of a small mayfly, the first I have seen this year, floating round the bend and on towards the shelving bank under the chestnuts. Its movement is inimitable. I watch it with bated breath as it rides the surface, quivers, rises, touches, and stays flittering on the surface. Surely my trout, if it has any spark of fire or sense of fitness, will rise to the occasion. Clear and slow and undisturbed by ripple, the water moves under the chestnuts' shade. Above, the sun of the late May morning moves to its zenith. Unaware of any world but its own, the mayfly skitters on the surface to its destiny. No trout moves. I hold my breath to no purpose. The fly moves out on the gathering current, round the bend and out of sight. No fish seems interested. I am not really surprised. The first mayflies, on this river at least, seem to go unscathed. It is as if trout have to 'come on' to this food. When they do they eat heartily, go mad. Even the biggest fish leave their secure lies to behave like youngsters. And afterwards, in late June when the fun is over and only the odd late mayfly appears, the 'pale omega of a withered race', it can cover a whole reach or two before it is taken by some gourmand hovering in an easy lie and still open to offers.

I have taken the hint that in a day or two the mayfly madness will be on, and for the moment must see what can be done with more modest temptations. I have seen one or two flies on the water and so move away from the bank to a place about twenty yards down, where I can manoeuvre my way across the river, very carefully, and stooping instinctively. I now have the shelving bank in my sights upstream. A line of barbed wire festoons the bank behind me, and bitter experience of being caught up in the backcast through not compensating for being four feet below bank level persuades me to move a yard or two upstream, so that my cast will be shorter. I flip the line once or twice up my side of the river, pitching it higher than normal on the backcast. The line fails to extend itself. Fear of being caught up behind has made me bring the rod forward a shade too soon. Next time it's better. Out of the corner of my eye, and with a slight hint from somewhere inside my eardrum, I sense that something has moved to the surface during the second or two when my attention was to the right, and on my false cast. I throw as delicately as I can about a yard upstream of the spot, and watch the fly riding the water slowly back downstream towards me. Nothing takes.

I let it come back almost to my feet in case a hasty withdrawal should disturb a fish which might take next time. I cast again. The fly alights a foot closer into the bank and moves back down towards me, even more slowly than before. A sudden twitch under it confirms that a fish is inspecting it. When there are few flies on the water, and the current is slow, fish are more choosy. In my experience, once a fly has been inspected at leisure in slow water by a trout he displays no further interest. Remembering this, while the fly is only a couple of feet from where it was tweaked I raise my rod slightly to remove slack between the fly and the rod tip, then tap the rod sharply, somewhere at the top of the butt end. The fly quivers slightly and it is taken instantly, as if the fish had been induced into making a choice by the unexpected movement of the fly. The rod bends as the trout makes for the water under the bank. I move him out, and gradually raise him to the surface. A minute or two with his nose out of the water and he comes to the net. Could it be last year's fish? The same perfect condition, about the same size, but no sign of a year's growth since last we met. It is probably a younger brother. This completes my bag for this beat. I place him with the first, close the bag, slip the net back on its strap, and ease myself across the river and up the bank.

I raise the sunglasses, and the bright gold of the morning floods my consciousness. A medley of sounds of which I was unaware while concentrating on my threshings and plyings delights my ear. Nature seems on holiday. The still air gives a limpid clarity to sights and sounds. 'You could hear a snail clear its throat a mile away..' I realise the truth of this comic evocation of a similar scene in the pages of Wodehouse, and smile again. Now that the morning session is over there must be a short interval, preferably in the village pub. 'Stay me with flagons,' I mutter as I rise and start to trek across the meadow. To tell the truth, neither beer nor ham sandwiches are important at the moment. My instincts tell me to make haste to the next beat beyond the village half a mile away and get on with it. But wisdom prevails. I must forget the river's temptations for an hour and remember the inner man. Too often I have reversed the order, and dragged my waders back long miles eight hours later, empty, weary, wrist aching, sharp prickles down my waders lodging between my toes. But not today. Today must be evoked as a model of angling bliss, so common sense must prevail.

Follow me to the car, whose bumper gleams beyond the stile. Wait till I have shuffled off my waders, pushed the rod through the nearside window, its butt resting on the ledge at the back, and follow me up the rutted track and out onto the drive, carefully avoiding the heifer whose rump sticks out, tail swinging and switching at flies as she feeds on the lush grass that edges the track. Up into third gear, over the cattle grid, and on to the village. It's twelve-thirty by the church clock. I'll see you at the pub.

4

The War

From 1940 to 1947 I was in the army. So far as the fishing goes they were lean years. Only one or two incidents remain in my memory. They kept the idea of angling alive and stand out in my mind like a good deed in a naughty world.

I was stationed at Barton Stacey in Hampshire, and one day, quite unexpectedly, I came on the Test. It may seem strange, but at that time I had only the vaguest idea of its reputation. What amazed me the instant I saw it was the clearness of its water, the lushness of its bordering vegetation, and the incredible numbers of very large trout which my eye could spot for more than a hundred yards upstream from the bridge on which I was standing. Was this an exceptional wartime form of the Test, unfished and full of large trout? Or is it always like this? I have not seen it since, so I do not know. Those gondola-like fish still hang there in my memory, suspended as if in air.

One day when I was stationed in Iceland we were picking signal lines up by a large river. It was a landscape of granite and lava dust, and bogs where a bren carrier sank within half an hour. I saw large salmon in a pool below us, and decided that the next time I had the opportunity, I would be prepared. When next I went into Reykjavik I sought for whatever gear I could find. In spite of my fairly respectable command of Icelandic there was nothing doing. My next ploy was to ask Begga, the girl who taught me the language. She produced a fairly tough rod and reel. With these I prepared a makeshift outfit. I tore the foil from the top of a tin of fifty Capstan cigarettes, which were free issue to the troops, and attached it above one of the likeliest hooks, which I contrived to weight with a twist of copper. The artificer (known in Gunner units as the 'tiffy') provided twine.

A week or two later, with a free afternoon, I set off on a motorbike and arrived at the river in great hope. In such a wild place I was likely to see no human being within a radius of twenty miles, and as for licences, permission, and the familiar rigmarole, the war had cancelled all its relevance. We were there to stop the Germans from using the island as an air base, not to stop anglers from having a little sport. Above the pool, cut in its granite basin, were some shallow glides, with rough water running into them. I began tossing out my makeshift tackle, a mere hook with a flash of foil attached. Within a cast or two I had learnt how to get it out and manoeuvre it at varying depths through the water. As soon as I approached the pool from the glides, and had passed my fly over the slight fall I was into a large fish. Up and down for a hundred yards I ran with my fish, noting with delight the shallow edges on my side of the pool where it would be easy to beach my fish when the time was ripe. Out he came in one gleaming curve, then off like a tiger, me after him with the rod bent double. Then the rod broke, and he was off, with a foot of rod and about fifty yards of strong twine trailing behind him. That was the last of my fishing in Iceland. The weather hardened, everything froze, and no one was able, or even tempted, to stray far from the camp.

I have already described a similar incident in Italy during the Italian campaign, when the 'tiffy' rigged me up a rod from an aerial and I had a glorious half hour in the river by which our guns were in action. Another occasion comes to mind on Lake Maggiore. The war was over, and I was at last able to take leave with a friend from the other battery. We took a jeep up to Lake Maggiore and worked round to Pallanza, where we put up in a hotel by the lake. One day, from Isola Madre (or it may have been Isola Maggiore) we looked down from some rocks and spotted an enormous trout. It was then that we went back to the shop where we had seen some thin copper wire lines wound on something like football match rattles. To these were attached vibro spoons. With them we set off in a boat and rowed far out. The day was hot and thundery. We had heard tales of the lake's treachery, of sudden storms in which boats had been swamped by large waves, and even of a steamer sunk. We attached our wire holders to the side of the boat and paid the line out, rowing slowly so that the spinners would sink. Nothing resulted. I could see the gleam of the copper down in the water and was sceptical from the first. We decided to swim. We had been stationed on the Adriatic since the end of hostilities and had grown used to the salty buoyancy of the water in which you could almost lie and go to sleep. As soon as we were in the water it felt like lead, and we seemed to have to expend twice the energy we expected in order to move forward. After about ten minutes a squall got up, and large waves began to make visibility difficult. The boat seemed to have drifted away, and as we swam towards it we realised that we were making little headway. It then became a race to overtake the boat before we were too tired. By the time we made it we were exhausted, and it was minutes before we could summon the energy to climb over the side. As I heaved myself up at last I noticed that one of the spinners was caught in my companion's shorts – the only capture of the day.

A month or two later at Courmayer in the Alps, where we had been sent to stop the French from running arms into the Aosta valley, I was visited by a general. After years of wartime abstinence he was seeking some fishing on the day or two of leave he was taking. The Doire, a rushing river of melting snow flowed not many yards away, draining from the glaciers of the Monte Bianco range and the Col de Ferret and Col de la Seine. In the evening he showed me some salmon flies he had kept with him in a wallet all through the war. We consulted a local on the advice of some of the villagers, and he lent us two rods. Our brief sorties to the river and our encounters with the trout of the Italian Alps will be described in another chapter.

5

Apprenticeship

It was in the Yorkshire Dales, Wharfedale to be precise, where my trout fishing apprenticeship proper began. One day I met the son of a farmer whose acres lay on an offshoot of the Wharfe, the Skirfair, just beyond Grassington. He told me I had only to proceed to the given spot, and I could fish to my heart's content. I set off, took the tiny lane bordered by loose drystone walls, and found myself in a valley broad and full of the sound of trickling water. On my right the limestone cliffs rose above the valley. A figure beside a large stack of cow manure answered to the name of the man I was seeking. Yes, he was the farmer, and yes, his son had mentioned me with regard to fishing. I shall never forget his words. 'Tha can fish theer as much as tha likes. Get down theer nah. There's a nice drop o' watter runnin.' I needed no further bidding.

The river was quite full, pebble-bottomed, varied as you could wish with bends, runs, riffles, shallows, pools and freshets for the angler to disport in. I had a second-hand fly rod, a few flies, no landing net and no skills to speak of. I had flicked for practice in the garden at home, read fly-fishing books by the dozen, and would not have aspired to even thinking of trying with a dry fly. This was wet fly country, and I was about to sample it for myself. In the course of that day I surprised even myself. It was possible. I could get the fly out and draw it across. What a feeling of triumph it was when I brought in my first half-pounder, a gleaming, spotted beauty which, as happens so often in such rocky streams in the north, took my fly on the opposite side the moment it started moving into the current. It was nothing in those days to hear of an angler taking forty fish from the Wharfe and its tributaries. The idea repelled me. That day I took dozens, but kept only four. I loved the wetness of the valley, the sense of water trickling everywhere in that limestone country. That river haunted my imagination all the time I was not fishing it. I was a busy man, with a job which occupied me by day and night, and my visits were rare but precious.

As yet I was not glutted enough with taking trout to eschew all means other than fly. I acquired a spinning rod, the one I mentioned earlier in speaking of the fallow season, and became quite expert at handling a quill minnow. Of all the artificial spinners, the quill minnow is the most delightful to look at and the most effective in fast water. The quill body is painted with blue and red spots. The tiny flight in its nose turns it nicely in the fast current, and it has that translucent quality that probably constitutes its main effectiveness. It never creates a furore in the water, or behaves like a turbine. Moreover, it is light enough not to sink too fast in shallow water. Cast across and drawn back under the banks it is, in my experience, deadly. I learnt how to make my own quill minnows. Speaking of it has given me the urge to fish with it again. Now that I think of it, I know a part of the Teme at Skyborry where, on a hot day in midsummer, everything else being hopeless until dusk, it will be exciting to try one. The river there is very like the Skirfair. I can hardly wait.

The places I gradually became acquainted with from my base in the market town at the centre of Wharfedale are all as sweet-sounding to me as the waters themselves:.Arncliffe, Grassington, Linton, Star Bottom, Burnsall, Appletreewick, Barden Tower. And there are always miracles, even in waters where the average fish is only half a pound. Once, fishing at Appletreewick, I heard that a trout weighing twelve pounds had been shot with an airgun at Starbottom. There was hardly any water in the river, which runs very low in the height of a dry summer, but he had been spotted in a hole and done to death in this ignominious manner. I think my facts are correct, but anyone who wishes to confirm them may do so, I believe, for the fish, I was told, was to be kept. The next time I am in those parts I shall look him out in the nearest pub.

After so many days as a child starved of a fishable river, and confronted with forbidding notices such as 'Private Water, 'Fishing strictly Reserved', 'No Fishing', it was wonderful to find so many places where a day's fishing could be had for a few shillings, or by simply asking the owner of the riparian rights. The public house at Appletreewick on the little road running above the Wharfe provided such day tickets in those days, and probably still does. There is wonderful fishing there. I have already mentioned the winter grayling, and the frosty day when we stood on boulders above a deep pool and took fish with flies in a burst of sun. Fold Farm, just upstream from the pub water, and sprawling about fifty yards above the river, used to own the fishing on a roaring stretch of water debouching into a large grayling pool. I came across it by accident.

I had two or three days' holiday. By this time I had moved to Wallasey, and was suffering from my familiar fishing starvation. My wife urged me to go to the Dales, where she would join me in a few days when her holiday began. I set off, bought a licence in Gargrave, memories wakening in me, then proceeded up the Wharfe to Appletreewick. The rain was streaming down. It was tea-time, and I was hungry, and needed to find a place to stay for a few days. I drove down to Fold Farm and asked the kindly farmer's wife if she knew where I could stay. She suggested a place nearby, with a hint that they were rather particular about mealtimes, and told me that if I didn't like it, I could come back and she would see what could be done. I did not find the place at all to my liking, so I returned to the farm and was invited inside. It was an outside privy, she explained, but they had fishing on the river and she showed me a sweet, hay-smelling room where I would sleep. She understood the ways of anglers, and said I could have breakfast whenever I liked, a packed lunch, a meal whenever I wanted it in the evening, and supper whenever I returned after the evening's fishing. I rejoiced inside as she said she would do something for me that moment, so that I could get off to the river for an evening's fishing. I ate a delicious meal in the parlour, which was full of well-chosen antique furniture (in which she turned out to be very knowledge-able). An hour after my arrival I was off to the river, her instructions in my ears, to ply my much-neglected rod once more in the waters of the Wharfe. The rain was thinning, and a gush of sunlight was flooding the valley as I wove my way up the banks, savouring the familiar sense of water running everywhere, underground, through pebbly inlets and over smooth boulders. There was a stretch of about three hundred yards of tumultuous water, all of which I would fish meticulously the next day. Then, as I recall, the river smoothed out and widened, gliding over smooth, flat pebbles, moving deeper under the far bank which was overhung by a large, well-grown tree. After that it narrowed again and romped down a slope into a large, deep pool, the grayling pool of which the farmer's wife had spoken.

My first discovery, apart from the fact that the river was full of trout, was that to wade slowly downstream was a perilous business. The surface of the submerged boulders was like ice, and my rubber waders skidded at every step. Moreover, to stride over large boulders was to risk landing in a hole waist deep. It seemed that there were fish in the slack behind every other one. That evening I tried only sample places in the torrent, took several fish, and then made for the bottom of the rapids, where the river broadened. Here I could wade over smooth, flat pebbles in about a foot of water, and cast my flies (a dropper and a tail fly, both Greenwells, the dropper touched with a fly flotant) under the large tree where the water was deeper and glided smoothly, with no ripple. This kind of spot is always a favourite with me, and I always seem to do the right thing. As dusk was beginning to take away the light from the watery sun, the trees still dripping occasional salvos, I moved slowly out in the shallow water. I crouched as low as possible, enjoying the beauty of the even pebbles and the glow of brown they shed through the clear, pulling water. A cast or two and the flies are drifting under the bank (I avoid the branches by a horizontal cast over the surface of the water). A second or two, and the dropper is taken. The trout oars lustily upstream, but he is soon coming to the net, flat on the face of the shallow water. A few minutes later the same thing is repeated two yards downstream at the same spot.

I decided to leave the grayling pool to end my next day's fishing, and returned to the farm. Coffee, a chat with the farmer and his wife, then bed. From what they say, I gather that grayling are considered much better eating than trout, so I am hoping that I shall have plenty of both to offer them tomorrow. My evening's catch, and whatever else I take will be left with them. Sleep comes, and I wake early, the smell of fresh Dales' water coming through the open window.

It will be noticed how often in these jottings I lapse into the present tense. The reason is simple. As soon as each memory grows into detail, I feel as if I am reliving the experience. In any case, a moment-by-moment narrative seems to call for it. So here I am, up and about, collecting my rod, having breakfasted royally, a packet

of sandwiches in my pocket and glad that the day is bright. These moments stand out in memory as clearly as the adventures at the river. They are part of that thrilling world of anticipation that all true anglers will recognise. One of the minor pleasures of my present situation is that when I returned last night I left my rod by the wall, and merely have to take it in my hand, already mounted and ready for the fray. Again, there is that Dales' feeling of running water, under my feet, afar and near. I drink in the sweetness of the morning, a mixture of moorland bracken and exhaling wetness as I walk down the few hundred yards to the river.

I go to the top end of the runny stretch, and spend virtually the whole morning combing every inch of it until I have reached the shallow glides. It is absorbing work. The boulders over which the torrent creams are backed by sinks where the water is deep enough to deter the wader. I cast across, mend line, then do my best to slow the sweep of the flies downstream. Raising the rod helps, and by paying off slack from the reel, I keep the flies dancing rather than dragging. Takes are frequently on the far side as the current draws the cast and moves the flies from the slacker water. Playing fish against the current is difficult, but I soon have several in the bag. As I tune in to the ways of this stretch, I discover that it is best to comb the near water below me first. There are taking trout behind the large boulders. By casting short, rod up, I can drift the flies without involving much of the line. This way I take fish which would otherwise be 'lined' on the retrieve had I begun by casting across to the other side first. Within an hour, in spite of all my precautions, water has entered the tops of my waders and my legs are wet. But it is warm work, and I feel no undue discomfort.

The high peak of the morning comes towards the bottom of the stretch. In midstream, in a relatively calm pocket, I see a fin break the surface as my flies pass. I try again. My rod bends sharply. I must be into something heavier than the others. I find it difficult to move the fish. It seems to hold against the current. I have to move down to him, winding in. It takes me five minutes to bring him to the side. As he approaches I see what has happened. I am foul-hooked into the dorsal fin of a grayling of over a pound. My flies swept past and caught the fin I saw on the previous cast. No wonder I had a struggle, but the farmer's wife will be pleased. The fish is virtually 'drowned' by the time I take him off the hook through being drawn backwards against the current. I bag him and light a pipe. Time to pause and take refreshment. I walk up the meadow to the pub and eat my sandwiches to the accompaniment of lunchtime music from the radio inside. The draught Guinness goes down like wine. After the roar of water in my ears for so long, everything seems strangely peaceful and quiet. I saunter down the moorland road to the bridge at Burnsall. Lovely water. I resolve that some day I shall endeavour to fish that wide, curving, pebbly stretch, with its glides and crisping runnels.

Up to the top end of my stretch again. I find a place to cross just above the limit, and fish it down from the other side. Again I am rewarded at intervals with takes. I have enough trout in the bag, so I return the afternoon fish to the water. After the evening meal I descend with eagerness again to discover the grayling pool. The river narrows and rushes with a marked fall between high banks to the pool, which spreads before me in a maze of currents and eddies. I am no expert in the ways of grayling, so with modest caution I decide not to 'spoil' the water before I have sized it up. I take off the Greenwells which have served me since I arrived and mount a small hackle red spinner and a red spider. Again I place a touch of flotant on the dropper and drift them down the main current by dropping my cast short. About the centre of the pool the flies are pulled sharply down and for the first time in my life I am into a 'double'. As they weave and jerk, I know that the fine leader must part. It is the tail fly that breaks. I land the remaining fish, and it joins the other fish in the bag. I am pleased. It proves that both flies are being taken. I replace the leader. The red spider has to be succeeded by another red spinner. I drift them down again. For the rest of the evening there is no sign of interest until just on the edge of dusk, when the bob fly, drifting just below the surface, sounds suddenly and another grayling joins the others in the bag. The two taken from the pool are about three-quarters of a pound each. I trudge back up to the farm to hand over the day's takings to the farmer's wife. Before I show them, she tells me the number and rough weight of the fish I took in the river earlier. When I am puzzled, and begin to credit her with occult powers, she tells me that she looked in my bag at the door while I was eating my meal earlier. We drink milk coffee while I recount the day's events. In bed, as I fall asleep, I seem to hear the roar of water, and in the darkness I seem to be drifting down the surface of the Wharfe, still plying my rod.

I have two more memories of Wharfedale and the days of my first fly-fishing. The first concerns a lesson that went sharply home, so clear and undeniable was the evidence offered. I was watching a man fishing in a reservoir (called 'reservoy' in Yorkshire). He was casting a float and hook baited with maggot. In the ten minutes while I watched, he took as many trout, all of about three-quarters of a pound. When he broke, and I went up to talk, he showed me the tiny hooks he was using. The next size bigger, and a five-pound instead of a three-pound breaking strain cast, he said, and he would never have a nibble. Seeing my slight scepticism, he put on a size fourteen hook, with a slightly heavier cast, and for the next ten minutes his float remained with no sign of a bite. To prove his point, he then reeled in, replaced the small hook and lighter cast, attached a maggot, and for the next ten minutes, again took as many fish. Obviously there was a shoal of fish where he knew them to be, but there was no doubt that his maggot, seen in the shoal with a slightly larger hook and cast, was refused by every fish. This object lesson remains with me to this day, and when fly-fishing I bear it strongly in mind. So often has my luck changed when I have replaced a leader and fished lighter, especially in lakes and slower, clearer waters.

My other memory goes back to the days when I still had hopes that my wife would catch the disease and, if introduced to the right approaches, might become madly intoxicated like myself. To live in paradise alone seemed selfish. She had accompanied me once or twice, it is true, but I attributed her lack of excitement when the rod bent to the fact that she was not holding the rod. I decided that she should be given the tackle in her hands, and positioned in the right place at the right time. Once she caught her first fish the spell would be wound up and she would be hooked for life. There had been rain higher up in the valley, and the Wharfe, a quick riser, was already covering some of the tufts and boulders my eye had marked. Flurries of coloured water were tingeing the current. I selected a spot behind a large bank where the deepening water was circling nicely, mounted the spinning rod, and after she had been given a few shots for practice further down, left her to spin the eddy. Minutes later, from my position fifty yards away, I heard a cry. I rushed down the bank to find her peering through her fingers her face a picture of horror, at the ground before her. The rod lay flat. A few yards away in the grass a three-quarter pound trout was threshing and leaping. I despatched the fish, hooked up the spinner, and awaited the expression of wonder and triumph that I fully expected would now transfigure her face. Instead, I saw horror and revulsion still. Since that occasion long ago she has not had a rod in her hands. On the rare occasions when she accompanies me at the river for an hour or two, she will do her duty for a minute, then retire to a comfortable spot and lose herself in a book. Even the capture of a trout will not distract her, and when I rejoin her, she gives my captures the barest token of attention. I have concluded that her archetypal blueprint lacks the vital trigger where response to fishing is concerned. She points out that my own blueprint is equally lacking in trigger mechanism where dresses and shoes in women's shops are concerned, and I can only agree.

6

The Upstream Worm

It was in the Yorkshire Dales that I first discovered the pleasures of using the worm without a float, cast on a short line upstream. The Skirfair, of which I have spoken, was ideal for this delightful alternative to fly-fishing. It has low, open banks, and can be waded easily in midstream.

My own choice for this kind of fishing is a longish, soft rod. Too stiff a rod tends to jerk more worms off the hook than is acceptable even to the upstreamer. With the right rod, and a goodish supply of worms, stored overnight in moss soused in milk, so that they are supple and rubbery, the angler sets off to such a river as the one I have described and begins his deadly work. He crouches as low as possible and works his way to the centre of the little moorland river. He knows that because of the shallowness in the middle, the main body of fish will be lying in the edges on this particular day. It is, for preference, just clearing after a rainy night, and the water has a purposive singing sound in its voice. In places the river will have risen, and even an inch will have made a difference to the supply of food washed down the edges over the smooth brown pebbles. His aim is

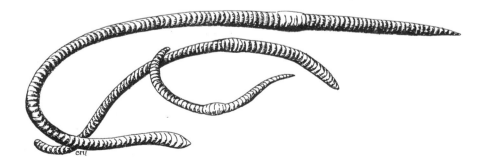

to work his way up the stretch, a yard at a time. First he casts up and under the right bank ahead of him two or three times, then similarly to the left. It is tiring work. In the faster parts of the stream his arms and hands are hard at work all the time. He casts as gently as possible, sees the worm kiss the water ahead and disappear, then he is pulling back the slack as fast as possible as the worm eddies and sinks with the current. He fishes it back almost to his feet, then casts again. After an hour, the most experienced angler needs a short break from his wrestle with the stream bearing ever down against him.

But the rewards for getting the knack are rich. At the end of the hour he has four nice trout to show for his pains, and he has moved only a matter of forty or fifty yards upstream. The advantage of this kind of fishing in a river such as this is that, with luck, the trout are being approached from behind, so that the visibility problem is diminished. Fishing a wet fly downstream to these same fish puts the angler into a more exposed position, and when the stream is narrow, as this is, he must walk down the opposite bank in order to get decently across and not merely down to the fish. This, then, excludes from his pursuit a whole head of fish under the unfished bank. No use trying the trodden bank later. The fish are down.

Upstream worming then, can be a decent addition to the trout angler's repertoire. Once the initial irritation of constantly losing the worm is avoided by the tricks of experience, a whole world of possibility is opened up. My own ploy is to swing and lob, rather than 'cast' the worm as·if it were a fly. I bring it round as far to my left or right as convenient, then swing it up under the bank ahead, shooting a yard of line as I do so. In this way I drop the worm with little splash, and gain a little distance.

Less demanding uses of the worm in the Dales are when the river is rising, or is just clearing away after it has been in spate. The angler arriving at the river, finding the fly unproductive, attaches hook and worm to his cast, ties a feather on as a float, and swings into some eddy, the water being so coloured that visibility is no longer a problem. This kind of situation has its charm. It takes us back to boyhood days. We wait, see the float disappear, and tighten in expectation. Wet-fly rivers of the north, especially those which rise and colour frequently, are the right places to ply the work when the fly can only fail. An alternative is the quill minnow, mentioned elsewhere. Cast down the banks, even in the fastest water, it always produces results – or nearly always.

These are the rightful and permissible alternatives open to the fly fisher of the northern streams. I make for myself one proviso. I set my limit according to the stream. Naturally, in 'Fly Only' waters I abide by the rules. Elsewhere, I fish as my inclination indicates, but I never take more than my share of fish. In the pub nearby, where I repair at lunchtime for a drink, the landlord tells me he once took 'fotty' fish from just below a certain bridge when the river was clearing after a flood. That, to my mind, is greedy. The good angler should not overplay his hand when the dice are falling right.

7

Pike and Trout in the Chislet Marshes

The Stour valley below Canterbury opens up after Fordwich, the home of the special 'Fordidge trout' of Izaak Walton. It flows broad and slow below Westbere Lakes, which border the river. On one side are old gravel pits, long since matured into fine fishing grounds, full of every kind of coarse fish. Here and there are tongues of narrow water like lagoons, bordered with reeds and rushes. From these lakes years ago, large pike were taken every season, to say nothing of carp, bream and the rest. The great advantage of these lakes was that they bordered the river. On a sharp winter or autumn day, armed with a spinning rod and pike spoon, you could walk for miles along the river spinning for pike or perch, and fish the lakes all the way back. One afternoon in late October I had fourteen size-able pike from the lakes. I attempted to catch the feeling of that afternoon in the following poem, published in *The Countryman* years later.

October Pike

I walk with death in my hand and peace in my heart
Through morning gold by the old October lakes
Where the sky lies late in bed thinking of nothing
But summer, and blue, and what she will wear today.
The sun wades up to his waist in her languid hours
Opulent and replete but unassuaged
In his lusty ways, and she gives in her plenitude
As I walk with them all the way up to the zenith.
It is all love and death this morning. The pike
Lances me with his eye and electrifies
To rabid assault in the lily-beds where he was spawned
To murder and die with a silver spoon in his mouth.
He grew to be bully of the kindergarten
Loitering with intent in the muddy slums,
A teddy-boy with a razor in his teeth
When I spotted him on my beat and ran him in.
Upstairs they are still at their beautiful lechery,
But an hour or two in October can turn a moral.
By mid-afternoon he will drown in the golden lake
And a juvenile wind will have slashed her all to pieces.

When there was nothing doing with the spinner, which was rare, you could trot a bait down the river, using the longish spinning rod and end-line reel, and have plenty of sport. One day in winter, the countryside agleam with frost, and a thin layer of ice tinkling under my waders, I swung out my spoon for its first cast of the morning, and as soon as it touched the water a large pike rushed at it. I lost that fish, but the spoon, made of tougher metal than nowadays, was bent at a right angle. If the pike were stirring in neither river nor lake, I would sometimes go to the places in the lagoons where on previous occasions I had had successful encounters. It was thrilling to cast the spinner along to the end of the clear spit of water, and see it sink among the spinneys of tall weed that bordered the 'clearing' in the submerged forest. Often the pike I had taken a week ago would rush from its covert, and after ten minutes renew my acquaintance on the bank. I had the same pike from the same place several times, and took care to note the markings of all the pike I wrested from the lagoons on future occasions.

In those days I lived by the river a mile or two upstream from

Canterbury. For the price of a rod licence, the 'city water' being free, you had a mile of wonderful trout water to fish. The river then ran on, gin-clear, under the willows of the Westgate gardens. During the season my activities were confined mostly to the city water. The stretch above it was club water, but in the open stretch that was free, the conditions, with the ideal blend of weed and gravel, left nothing to be desired. The blue-winged olive hatched in great numbers and I fished almost exclusively with it, except at dusk when the sedges were being guzzled by big trout at the edges. Occasionally, when there was nothing to be done with a fly or nymph, I would go to the Westbere marshes and try for sea trout. On a June evening, the water low, the temperature high, I would find myself at dusk on a stretch of open bank, the river wide, about a mile above Fordwich. With a black spider, smallish, or a brown nymph on the point, I would begin to fish on the edge of dusk, casting far out, mending the line, and letting the fly come slowly round, occasionally hand-lining to impart a tempting twitch to the offered morsel.

Sea trout have exceptionally good eyesight, hence the need for a long cast and care in manoeuvring the fly. If the taking fish is fresh run, and has not been in the fresh water for more than two or three weeks he generally feeds voraciously, and the fly will hook without need for a strike. It helps to keep the rod up when bringing the fly round, so that when a fish takes, a constant pressure can be exerted. Because of their soft mouths this is essential, but even so many fish manage to rid themselves of the fly, or it is pulled out by the use of too much pressure. When sea trout have been in fresh water for several weeks they feed less avidly, but still show interest in a temptingly offered fly. These fish often come to the surface and struggle. The best treatment seems to be to give slack, then renew the pressure. Sometimes during the taking time they twitch at the fly, take it, but run in with the line so that contact is lost. A sideways strike is often advised on these occasions, but on some evenings of many such takes, the results are few fish in the bag. I never fished after dusk with more than one fly. I find from bitter experience that if the dropper is taken there are difficulties when the fish come to the net. The fly on the point gets tangled in weeds, or rushes, or the net and valuable time is lost in freeing it. There is a period lasting for about two hours on summer nights of fishing for sea trout when things happen, if they happen at all. After this, unless you are prepared to wait till dawn there is little sport.

One of the pleasures of this part of the river was that there was no call for the purist approach. Upstream from Fordwich, right on past Canterbury to Thannington Without, where my lawn ran down to the river under stately willows, the Stour was definitely a trout stream. Its mixture of weed and gravel was ideal for spawning, and the brown trout with which it teemed were short, fat, and always in fine condition. I rarely took one under a pound, and I had many of two, three and four pounds. It was sad to hear, a few years ago, that a paper-mill a mile or two above Thannington had polluted the water and ruined the trout fishing. Below Fordwich, however, things were different. The river broadened, and there was a sense that it was hastening on to more serious appointments than those it had had so far in its course – flirtings with trailing willow streamers, footbridges and stone stanchions – and would soon be dressing itself for its betrothal to the sea. In addition to the odd trout and sea trout, it harboured a complement of coarse fish: pike, bream, perch and eels.

So, on a July day when the trout were not rising upstream of Canterbury, a few miles downstream, below Fordwich where Izaak Walton had noted the prognathous, ferox-like trout of immense size, you could walk for miles along the river, the lakes to your left, and take your choice between the two. The beat was a familiar one to me. It ran past Westbere, perched up an escarpment above the river, where I had bought a house when I first went to live near Canterbury. On the lawn in the garden was a signal pine, tall as a ship's mast, which could be seen for miles. Conrad had once lived in the village. Nearby, looking across the valley there was a house built on the site of a Roman villa. Its flanking drives were massed with blooming rhododendrons in the spring, and the whole frontage, its back to the village road, was hung with wisteria. There, on a summer evening, I would repair when the mood took me, on my way back from a skirmish for sea trout in the river below. I would sit in the circular rose garden, which was enclosed by a yew hedge ten feet high and six feet thick, and chat with the charming old lady about Edward Thomas, fishing, and whatever came to mind. Drinking a glass of sherry there one evening, and clasping the latest book she insisted that I *must* read, she told me she had learnt Russian when she was seventy. Her vivacity, her enthusiasms, gave her a girlish quality and a delicate grace I always now associate with those fishing evenings. In return for a brace of trout she would dispatch her husband, a gentleman of equal charm but more practical bent, to the greenhouses, and he would return with a bouquet to take home and, always, a special orchid from his cherished collection. He showed me a toga pin, a beautiful artefact in gold that he had found in the garden. We always took a walk along the balustrade (along which, at nearly eighty, he had planted a close yew hedge as a hostage to the future he would never see) then turn down and tour the series of sheltered little wolds he had planted with apple trees. In that perfect position the Roman owner, no doubt, had had his terraces of vines, and perhaps had sat drinking his wine where we had sipped our sherry. Far from his native Italy, legionary, impresario, diplomat or trader, I am sure he would have little cause to regret in this particular outpost of the empire. Looking down the sheltered slopes across the broad river valley, doubtless with Ovid's elegies from Tomi in mind, he would count his blessings.

Such memories confirm my conviction that fishing is all a matter of association and context. Who would ever carry the torch for long if it were merely a matter of hooking a fish and pulling it in? Memory encapsulates, filters, excludes and edits. My memories of the valley just below Westbere are always of hot evenings and dusk fishing. Nearer to Fordwich, they change to winter, and spinning for pike. One of the lakes carries an image of a golden October day, the sun in a rosy haze as pike after pike ravens at my spoon. One day in December, a wintry sun glinting on a thin covering of ice, we walked barefoot across a waterlogged meadow, enjoying the feel of it, and the light crunch of the wafer-thin ice crinkling at our ankles. I carried someone on my back. That was at Fordwich, and the name always brings it back.

I shall say something later about the delight of not being a purist or a fishing snob. Armed with a small wooden plug, blue, with red spots, I would explore this broader Stour when the blue-winged olive was not on the water above Canterbury. It ran wide and even-paced. In summer, the weed was still well below the surface in those days. I would cast across to the other side and watch every dart and zigzag of this little miracle of a plug as it came round and up and back towards me. It was like a live thing in that current. But try it in stiller water, and its performance was a washout. Often I would see a trout follow it all the way back to the rod-tip, its nose right up to the plug, the gyrations involved unbelievable. Every cast was a sheer delight. And the rewards, on many occasions, were abundant. Two-pounders by the score I have taken from that stretch, and many a three-pounder. It was unlike any other kind of spinning. There was never any danger that the plug would plummet. It stayed an inch or two under the surface, and its to-and-fro oscillations and dartings were frenetic. Following trout were mesmerised. Even with the plug at the very tip of the rod, a trout which had followed it from the middle would remain for as long as twenty seconds before sheering away disappointed at the now inert simulacrum. One daring and hungry trout paused with its nose at the plug, which was hanging a mere couple of feet from the rod-tip. I remained as still as a statue. With a sudden peevish motion it darted the plug into its mouth and was taken. This kind of spinning had all the delight of fly-fishing in clear water. You could see the whole progress of the plug from mid-river. It seemed as if the actual movement of the tiny plug was irresistible, and lured the trout as it darted above them.

Another pleasure in certain parts of this reach was spinning for perch. And when all else failed, I would saunter along, trotting a worm down under the banks...worm, float and me a few yards behind. The progress was halting, but the process pleasurable, and on more than one occasion I would haul out a trout in places where they could not be taken by any other means. Here and there, down beyond Westbere, there were deeper parts, holes where the river ran tumid, and here on occasion I would live bait for pike, always returning them intact after the struggle. In this part of the river, of mixed population, this was right and proper. Above Canterbury it was a different matter. There the trout was sacred, and any jacks that took were instantly removed.

Always, when I had gone downstream so far, and I sensed that the river had changed its character and had really smelt the sea, I turned back. It had no charm for me in its sea aspect. For me the sylvan stream, the shallow reaches, the visible underwater scene were what constituted the charm of the river. How heartening on the way back to see it gradually regain its inland nature. Perhaps it was a memory of boyhood frustrations. The only river accessible to me then was the Wyre, which drained the Fylde. It was a tidal river, of deeply dredged muddy banks where you fished on the bottom with a paternoster. Its blear aspect at Shard Bridge was always disheartening to one who had seen the Wye, and drunk the milk of paradise in its reaches. So I eschew tidal rivers. Stony, weedy, gravelly or sandy bottoms are the river furniture for me. And my greatest delight is in the faster currents, the riffles over cobbles, the glides and creamings over boulders. But every man to his taste. I know there are addicts of straight dykes and sluggish waters, where the prey is all-important and the process less so. I see in memory all those lines of blue-overalled Frenchmen sitting along the banks of the Seine with their long poles, dawn to dusk. But I tell myself, 'Think not of them, thou hast thy music too.'

8

Catching the Disease

How did my addiction begin? I believe I was programmed from the beginning to respond to the mystery of water ... ponds, lakes, rivers and their aquatic life. If I see a bridge over a river or brook, I must hang there, peering into the water. The other day, the first of November, I was showing a friend the river where I fish, and as I hung over the bridge a few miles above the village, a kingfisher swooped along and under the parapet. Bridges flash like that kingfisher into my memory, far too many to mention. There remain a few which I believe have a permanent place in my iconography. One is the suspension bridge over the Wye at Foy above Ross. I shall focus on this elsewhere. Another is the bridge over the Monnow at Monmouth. After these there are dozens: the stone bridge over the brook at the cottage; the bridge over the river at Brampton Bryan; the bridge over the Doire at Ponte San Martino in Val d'Aosta; a certain bridge at Bekesbourne and the bridge over the Wyre at St Michael's. Then there are those two bridges over the narrow part of the lake in Stanley Park; the bridge with its V-shaped standing points at Leintwardine; Kerne Bridge; one or two bridges over the Granta between Queen's and King's Colleges, and all the bridges over the Wharfe between Bolton Abbey and Grassington. But I realise as I write that always when I look over bridges into the water below it is to peer at fish, or to search the water for signs of fish. Hence, my love of fishing must pre-date my fascination with bridges.

I think it all began on sunny days by a special pond at Staining, where older boys would display their catch in buckets. The tench, so big that it had to bend at the bottom, fascinated me. We took turns at dipping our hands in to feel its slimy heaviness. From the root of the willow tree, which provided a perfect platform from which the deeps of the pond could be searched with our eyes, we fished with our bent pins, lowering them into the depths and seeing the tiddlers attacking the dangling worm. It was by those ponds of the Fylde, which we all called 'pits', that the disease really took hold of me in my later boyhood. In those parts the farmers were fierce and loud of voice. Since then I have never heard one raise his voice in other parts of the country. Perhaps it's because I'm older and do not trespass. They were a force to be reckoned with in those days. Their dogs were always half savage, and seemed to depend for their nourishment on frequent nibbles at the calves of small boys.

The Fylde is a windswept square of land, bounded by the Wyre to the north and by the Ribble to the south. Once a great flat of water covered it. All that remained of this was a large mere ringed with a twenty-foot wide necklace of bulrushes. It lay below sea level, and had a sour surround of bog. It was the source of our mythology in those days. Fantastic tales were told of its finny denizens and their capture by people we never met directly. One day I discovered in the local library an account of six six-pound tench (mentioned elsewhere) taken one day towards the end of the last century in the mere. This remained in my mind, confirmed the mere as rooted in history. I thought that if there were fish of this size in the mere in the last century their size must be proportionately increased by now. One day when we saw an otter, and another when a kingfisher flashed on our sight, I knew that this was a place whose mystery would remain unplumbed. The fact that the mere could only be properly seen from the slightly higher ground a few hundred yards away, and that when you reached the ring of bulrushes at its edge it was effectively veiled from sight increased the mystery.

It was only decades later that I actually fished the mere. My brother had helped to erect an approach and had constructed a platform on the waterside of the ring of reeds. It was then that I looked over its surface for the first time. My brother had done a survey of the depth, had measured the acidity of the water, and accounted for the poor fishing compared with that of the previous century. We fished, but no putative monsters figured in our minds. A plague on all surveys say I. The pits of the Fylde were more attainable. They held roach and bream and tench and carp and eels. Since the rivers were beyond our reach, we depended on the pits for our fishing. Though at the time I regarded this region with the contempt we reserve for the too familiar, despising its lack of variety, its flatness and general harshness, I later came to place it and value it according to its type. When I had had my fill of hills and valleys, of clear rivers without signs of tidal influence, of lusher vegetation and gentler climate, I came to see my native Fylde for what it was, and to value it for what it had to offer.

In those days we would get up at four in the morning, creeping about so as not to disturb sceptical adults, who might descend and throw cold water on our enthusiasm. We would cross the last field to the selected pit with palpitating hearts, and thrill at the sight of water, reeds and ripples. How those ripples wrinkle their way through my memory still. I can see the red-tipped little floats jigging slightly in the ripples created by the strong western breeze that blew eternally in those parts. We watched them for hours with passionate intensity, scarcely daring to take our eyes away for a second in case the longed-for 'bite' happened while our attention was distracted. Rarely, but so memorably, the float would bob once or twice, then disappear. Or it would quiver, then slide slowly down and away. Paste was our general-purpose bait. The mixed odour of cow-dung and fish took over our bait tins, our fishing bags, our persons. Sometimes, on summer evenings, the larks aloft, the stiff breeze for once asleep, those pits, the green turf and the hawthorn hedges became Arcadia. Though we never captured a sizeable carp, we dreamed of doing so, and every moment of those enchanted evenings was an agony of anticipation.

There was a village five or six miles away surrounded by thin copses and spinneys. They ran in narrow tongues, low on the west side, growing taller on the leeward side away from the prevailing wind. One day while trespassing in one of these spinneys we discovered a large pond, sheeny and black and sinister, dead leaves clearly visible on the bottom at the edges. Suddenly a heron took off from the other side of the pond, and we were left in no doubt that here was a treasure trove of fishing possibility. We departed almost as soon as we had arrived, planning a visit with the rods, and excitedly speculating. As it grew light the next morning we were propping our bikes in the hedge and making our way through the meadow to the spinney. How many times we paused to listen. For what? The sound of pursuing dogs? The voices of angry farmers? The morning's fishing remains in my mind as one of those rare occasions when hope is more than fulfilled. Scarcely had we approached and cast our floats on the water than they dived surely down and we were hauling out the largest roach we had ever taken. Hour after hour we hauled them out and popped them back. We smiled at each other in glutted delight. No wonder the heron kept the secret to himself. The pond was full of fish. Why did we never go there again? There is a blank in my memory. This should have become a regular goal in our fishing forays, but that was the sole visit we ever paid it. Years later I heard the local zoo had dredged it during the war to feed animals or other fish. It still holds a hallowed place in my memory. I can still smell its damp earthiness, see the heron taking off, its legs dangling, and the forbidding notice 'Trespassers will be Prosecuted!'

The tench at the bottom of the bucket, and the six six-pounders taken one day from the mere in its heyday call to mind another encounter with this fish years later. It was shortly after the end of the war, and I was driving down from Champoluc in the Italian Alps towards Turin. After the bracing air at six thousand feet the prospect of the heat of the plains in the height of summer was a daunting one. I stopped at a village on the edge of a long, deep-looking lake. Soon I was seated under a vine trellis at a table. I was told that a cool dish of soused 'tinca' with half a bottle of the local wine was what I needed. Aware that I was buying a pig in a poke, but charmed by the solicitude of mine host, I took my glass, and wandered to a large fountain across the piazza to await the arrival of the mysterious 'tinca'. The basin of the fountain, which was enormous, contained several hundredweight of fish, among them some of the largest eels I had ever seen. I stared at four or five fish of huge dimensions, and suddenly realised that they were tench. I was told that the lake was netted twice a week and had been so netted as far back as anyone could remember Suddenly 'tinca' clicked – it was the Latin (and Italian) name for my old friend of long ago in the bucket. With some doubt in my mind I returned to my table to eat soused tench. It was delicious, garnished with alpine mint, which they called 'glacial mint', and washed down with a second half-bottle of wine. Small wonder that in times past all thriving farms or country houses boasted a stewpond. The tench, now despised as a food fish, is indeed delicious, soused and garnished as I have described.

The Wyre at Shard Bridge was only a few miles from where we lived. But in those days it did not meet up with my requirements for what a river should be. On holiday at Ross, where my father was born, I had drunk deep of the charms of the Wye. I had haunted its wide-aisling meadows past Foy and Howcaple. I had walked its windings from Kern Bridge through English and Welsh Bicknor, and below the Seven Sisters, had followed it in its wanderings through the woods, and heard the salmon falling back like pigs into the water after their leaps. And I had watched a man with a two-handed fly rod casting a fly without letting it touch the surface. It was nothing to see three village boys walking along the bank, each with a salmon round his neck, head and tail in either hand. After such magnificence I was not old enough to appreciate the Wyre for what it was. At Shard Bridge it was tidal. Boats anchored with chains (which could not hastily be cut with a knife) were rapidly upended as the tide filled the steep mud banks where it narrowed, and my mother, as a warning, read fatalities aloud from the local paper. She was obsessed by the thought that I would drown in a pit, or in the Wyre. The dragging of pits for lost boys was a frequent occurrence in those parts, and I now regret my lack of understanding of her worries. We would take lobworms and paternosters and weights, and fling them into the muddy Wyre, and sometimes be rewarded by a few flatfish. But it was a cold, muddy, dirty job, and I longed for a countryside of hills, clear rivers and pebbly bottoms. A

friend went on holiday to the Lakes, and returned with news of a
river there – the Sprint. What a name for a runny river! I longed to be
there, or by the Wye ... anywhere but where I was. That was the prevailing sickness of my boyhood and youth and I had to live with it.

But there were compensations. St Michael's was about ten miles
away on the Wyre, with a stone church and a rural air. The Wyre
here had almost lost its tidal character and was the nearest thing to a
fishable river within our grasp. Thither we repaired one day, our
bikes laden, to camp for two nights. We had a tiny tent between us, a
thin groundsheet, a blanket each, and a blackened little stove we
could never light. We met a friendly doctor who came over from the
house as we put our tent up by the river and insisted on lending us
some horse blankets. We spent the rest of the day catching
sticklebacks. In the evening we cut off their spines and placed them
ready in a jar. Black from head to foot with our grapplings and
tinkerings at the nauseous stove, we clung together through the
intense cold of the night until we could endure it no longer, and
emerged at four in the morning to a meadow waist-deep in thick
white mist. We walked with chattering teeth to a bend in the river
where the banks were twenty feet deep. There we climbed down
and baited our treble hooks with a stickleback apiece, lip-hooking
them. Then, with a depth of six feet below the big corks we used as
floats, we cast them in. The live bait moved the corks slowly, yard
by yard over the surface of the bend, where the locals had said there
was a deep hole. Suddenly, my brother's cork was towed under
with several yards of line. He waited for what seemed an eternity,
then struck. He played that fish for about five minutes, knowing
that the gut was strong enough if the fish didn't get his scissors to
close on it. Eventually he was brought in. We stood gazing at the
largest fish we had yet bagged ... a young pike of four pounds or so.
We had no further luck that day or the next. When we set off for
home, black as sweeps, and breasted the ever-blowing westerly
wind, my brother, imagining the detailed account we would be
begged to give, carried triumphantly in front, tied to his handlebars,
the putrefying body of our capture. But life never lives up to anticipation. At the sight and smell of us we were ordered out of the
house, the pike was placed in the dustbin, and we were made to
cleanse ourselves ingloriously outside.

Winter night-lines supplied another titbit in our early fishing diet. When the gales blew strong inshore, and the sea could be heard from our beds a mile away, we got the urge to set night-lines. We would consult the tide tables and proceed out at low tide with two hundred yards of line to which we had attached thin snoods, about a foot in length, every two feet along its length. We would peg down the line, making sure it ran slightly oblique to the line of the water, so that the pull of the tide would be lessened. Then we would stick the bait on each huge hook – lobworms for preference – and wait until the incoming tide was covering the whole length. Then, a habit gained from bitter experience, we carefully sighted the location of the line against a point on the pier and another on the cliffs. Roughly eleven or twelve hours later we would rise in the dark and go to pick up our line and its attachments. One winter morning especially stands out in my memory. At three in the morning the wind of the previous day had died down, but everything was frozen hard. Even parts of the beach and some of the pools were hard with ice. The light of the hurricane lamp was eerie as we trekked over the frozen beach in our little island of light. It was too dark even to pick out the pier, and the sea was a presence only by its sound. As we walked our eyes grew accustomed to the darkness as we carefully avoided our pool of light which dazzled. The sea was uncovering the far end of our line when we spotted it. As we walked along its length the light gleamed on the frozen forms of flounders, plaice and codling. Almost every hook had a fish attached to it. It took us almost till dawn to collect, load the catch, and wind in the line. And for the rest of the day we were proudly calling on friends and neighbours by the dozen with gifts of fish. I have never forgotten the growl of the sea, the salt smell, and the gleam of those frozen forms in the sand.

The test of faith is that it should be exercised 'in the difficultest point' as Sir Thomas Browne states. It is certain because it is impossible was his credo. A holiday at Stratford-on-Avon when I was about twelve was such a test. My brother and I were assured that we would be allowed to fish in the Avon all day and every day for a fortnight. When we arrived with our bamboo rods, floats and hooks, and surveyed the long reaches of meandering, sunny river, and realised that it was ours for two long weeks, our spirits rose sky-high.

We found a place on the first day so much to our taste that we went there every day and fished from dawn to dusk. During the whole period we had not a single bite and took not a single fish. When I now think it over, of course, there could be many obvious reasons for this. We never ground-baited. We stuck rigidly to our home-made concoction of paste for bait. We did nothing to measure the depth of the pitch we were fishing, and nothing to explore other pitches. None the less, faced on the last day with complete failure so far as the capture of fish was concerned, we remained as eagerly optimistic as during the first hours. Our eyes never left our floats. A world of infinite possibility lay beneath them, and we anticipated with true faith the working of the magic hand of chance. Perhaps those starvation rations kept our appetites sharp and confirmed us in the determination to 'strive, to seek, to find, and not to yield'. When we returned home and consulted our books we found a thousand reasons to account for our failure, and this was enough. Given the chance, armed with our new wisdom, we would without hesitation, have returned to the scene of our holiday, seated ourselves in the same spot, and fished contentedly for another fortnight.

Perhaps some tales told by our father of his fishing exploits, now forgotten, or the smell of his bait tin, or the reels and remnants we discovered in his abandoned fishing bag may have been the first quickeners of the disease in our blood. Ponds, pits, mere and the tidal Wyre were there to increase the disease. Fishing for us was then float fishing. The trout was not within our reach in that flatland of bog oak and stiff westerly winds. How the lure of the fly took over is another story. Once my ichthyolatry was assured in general, my passion for the pursuit of trout followed. I can place exactly when and where it all began, and I knew that I should be 'else sinning greatly a dedicated spirit'. That moment on the Monnow Bridge was when it all began.

9

Trout and Other Pursuits in the Italian Alps

Val d'Aosta, which drains Mont Blanc on the Italian side, via Col de Ferret and Col de la Seine, and receives the rivers which flow from Monte Rosa through Aosta, and from the Graian Alps on the other side above Aosta, was one of the main routes out of Italy, in Roman times, to transalpine Gaul. Aosta commands both the Grand St Bernard Pass and the Little St Bernard, which debouches higher up the valley at St Didier, near Courmayeur where the great massif of Mont Blanc blocks the valley at Entreves. Traditionally, the valley was French. It was taken over by Italy in Mussolini's time, and just after the war, when we had been in action for the best part of twelve months, my battery was sent to occupy the valley. Our job was to patrol all the valleys on the right bank to prevent arms from entering the valley from France. For this we split up into troops. After a long war this was a sinecure. All we had to do was to secure a good supply of logs for burning throughout the winter, carry out the daily patrols (which involved one jeep, one officer and one driver) and to keep ourselves fit and happy.

The troops responded to this with enthusiasm. Provided the usual gun and equipment maintenance was done meticulously, the morning parade, with its minimal allocation of duties carried out efficiently, troops were free by midday. I decided, rightly, as it turned out, that there was no point in spreading the jobs thinly throughout the day. Instead, we held first parade at 6am, and once the log gatherers in the three-tonners had returned and stacked their loads, and a daily inspection of both troops and billets had been carried out, everyone was free to do what he liked. We laid on a variety of optional activities, and every night there was a dance or a party. These were seasoned troops, well aware that the continuation of such delights depended on themselves. Never were troops

more smartly turned out, more prompt on parade, more ready to
sweat their hearts out at the usual chores. Never was the list of those
'on a charge' smaller, or the sick parade so unnecessary. Happiness
reigned, and it was well deserved. Countesses, even duchesses, visiting their old haunts after so long, danced with gunners, bombar-
diers and sergeants in a carefree, post-war insouciance.

The reader will have gathered from the foregoing background
details that I, too, was not bowed down with any weight of responsi-
bility at this golden period, and for most of the day, almost every
day, I was able to breathe deeply, stretch out my arms, and say 'This
is the life!' – and mean it. I occupied a splendid alpine villa about
two hundred yards from the hotel where the troops were billeted.
The village was Courmayeur. It was set high above the river, surrounded by the scent of pinewoods, and there, towering above, all
the magnificent nearness of the Monte Bianco chain. The villa,
which I occupied in lone splendour, had been lavishly designed in
the alpine style. In a corner of the billiard room was a snug alcove
with a large window which looked out up to the slopes of Monte
Bianco. In the morning I ran the bath full of the icy snow water
which gushed from the taps, and plunged in regardless of the shock
that would follow. The summer sun, and the sharp mountain air,
the medley of pine green, blue sky and dazzling white, combined
with the sharp, resinous quality of the air made this a paradise. All
the fishing trips I managed in my leisure hours, alone in this world
of peace, so different from the white dusted heat and turmoil of our
days in action, are coloured in memory by the thrill of those days at
Courmayeur, queen of the brilliant Alps.

One or two incidents stand out. One day the general mentioned
in an earlier chapter phoned to ask if I could put him up for a day or
two's leave, and was there any possibility of fishing for trout on the
Doire. A little alarmed at what might be required of me, I duly
awaited his arrival, turned out the guard and called his attention to
the deserts of the war-weary lads who snapped to attention around
us. We looked at the billets, the guns, and noted the busy bustle of
trucks departing or unloading. When I broke the news that all
parades were over by midday he nodded his agreement and we
repaired to my quarters for a cognac and a planning meeting. By this
time I was beginning to realise that the man was decidedly human.

Within minutes he was producing from his kit a battered wallet crammed with trout and salmon flies, some of them dating back, obviously, to the Dark Ages. He was hungry to use them. The wallet had been with him throughout the war, and this was the first time he had had a chance to put its contents into action. His excitement was no greater than my own. I explained my famished state, told him of my foray with improvised tackle while we had been in action in the Serchio valley, and from that moment, no rank was pulled. We sought out a guide in the village, and consulted him. He said he could fix us up with a couple of rods by that evening. Out came the flies. He picked out the likeliest for the Doire, and advised us to clip down the hackles and wings. We spent the evening testing the casts we found in another of the general's wallets. I found some tinfoil from the stores, and we twisted it on the shanks of the selected flies, binding it with fine copper wire. By this time the general had shed his signs of office, and looked more like one of the local guides than a man of war.

Later in the evening an event took place that forever colours my memory of his visit. In the 'pineta' above the villa stood a wooden rotonda, a sort of bandstand, and that evening one of the locals was showing a film to an audience mainly of children and their mothers. At one point the film projector broke down, the film caught fire, and within seconds the whole place was ablaze. General panic ensued. There was screaming and shouting, and had it not been for the promptness of a couple of gun sergeants and a group of gunners who cleared the place, hauling and throwing out struggling groups of terrified people, there would almost certainly have been a disaster. By this time the pine glade was alight, and the troops dashed off for axes. What with the falling of burning trees and the inferno of the blazing bandstand, the wails and cries of the shocked spectators, the scene was like a film scenario. A ludicrous anti-masque ensued. Up through the glade came a shouting, gesticulating band of comic characters: the local fire brigade. They were dressed in braided tunics, hastily assumed, and great Roman helmets. They quarrelled every inch of the way, pushing the cart with large red wheels, which carried the hand pumps and the hose. Even when the hose was fixed and reeled out to the fire, they were disputing who should hold the nozzle, who should be at number two position, who should man this or that. Suddenly there was a cry of triumph. The water was arriving. All along hundreds of yards of hose, huge fountains of water spouted from myriad large holes. The two men standing like heroes holding the nozzle saw a tiny trickle of water fall from it over their feet. It was a scene of total farce. The gathered troops fell about on the grass roaring with laughter. The rotunda fell in. The sparks drifted high, and the crestfallen corps de ballet fell to quarrelling once more. Seeing the gun sergeant who had saved the situation with his cool promptness reminded me of a time in the Gothic line when his gun had had a blow-back during a barrage, (or so it was thought till he proved otherwise) and the whole gun was ablaze. I remember dashing up and seeing him pulling off Gunner L's clothes, which were alight, while the rest of the crew lay around the gun-pit, shocked and dazed. I have forgotten that sergeant's name, but him I do remember.

After parade next morning we went down to the river. The Doire was dancing from the ice field in happy mood. We found a place in the shadow of a cliff and fished all morning till lunchtime without a touch. There were no pools, and the river was a torrent sprinkled with large boulders. We let yards of slack drift down the river, holding the line in our left hands, so that in the event of a take, we would have enough slack to manoeuvre with. I left him to attend the midday parade while he sat wolfing down his rations, the stock of wine keeping cool in a little sink of water at his feet. On my way back, I decided that if the trout were lying behind the boulders, our flies were being swept away above them, too high and too fast. I consulted the general. It was about the pleasantest 'conference' I ever attended (and I attended hundreds during the Italian campaign) and the only one in which after 'Information' and 'Intention', 'Method' involved no crayoned markings on talc-covered maps, 'shoot down-to lines' or synchronisation. My plan was to fish more upstream, let the flies have a chance to sink with the line across stream, so that they could find their way into the sumps and sinks around the boulders. If this failed, I suggested that we should try wholly upstream, combing the boulders with a short line and dropping the fly like a nymph, raising our rods the while so as to let as little line as possible touch the water. In this way the fly would be dragged away less quickly, and have a chance to work more naturally.

We parted, and I began fishing about four hundred yards upstream of him. I marked a large boulder around which I guessed there would be a fairly deeply scooped sink, and keeping my rod as high as my upstretched arm allowed, cast the fly, plop, just ahead and to the right of the boulder, then off across to another. Remembering a salmon river in Iceland where, with improvised tackle, a tiffie-made hook and tinfoil fly I had hooked a large fish and almost played him out when the borrowed rod broke, I worked this one as quickly as possible to the side downstream and beached him. He must have been about a pound, almost white, the colour of the water. My heart pounded with joy. The war was really over. I despatched the fish and hastened down to the general with the good news that the method worked. Just as I approached, and he saw the fish dangling from a twig in my hand, he was taken by a fish behind a similar boulder, and a minute or two later he was beaching it downstream. We exchanged details – short cast, rod holding line out of water, letting the fly 'work' – and hastily parted again to resume our forays. We returned that evening glutted with the sport. Some of the trout went to the sergeants' mess, a couple to the guide who had obtained the rods, and my batman cooked ours over a wood fire in the trees outside. Sipping grappa with our coffee afterwards, we exchanged fishing stories and sat watching the snow-white slopes of Monte Bianco, now mysteriously blue in a suffusion of moonlight. We planned next day to explore further down the river, where it opened out into something resembling a pool. The general (who cursed solidly and fluently every time he hooked a fish, as if the adrenaline drew on some archetypal savagery in him) was euphoric, and since the confessional is sacred, I cannot enlarge on some of his more personal revelations. But he was companionable, and a very kind man. I showed him a couple of the poems I had written in action. When he left, unwillingly, on the third day, he generously handed over half the precious flies in his wallet, knowing I had none. Greater love hath no man. But I anticipate.

The next day I joined him after midday at the river, where he had captured a couple of brace, and we took the jeep down a mile or two, climbed out, and made for the pool. Again, we conferred. It was to be the shelf below the rocks for one rod, and the glide at the bottom for the other. We tossed for positions, and I was glad he got the shelf. After all, I would be there to fish it when he had merged into wherever he was going. From his wallet I chose a lean, clipped-down, nymph-like creature with a touch of red remaining, and went down to the glide. If there is one thing I love more than another in wet-fly-fishing it is searching the glide at the tail of a pool. In this case there was the added attraction that there was no need for concealment. The colour of the water took care of that. So as not to 'line' fish that might be nearest to me, I decided to explore the water fully, before extending my casts to midstream and beyond. As I began casting, the general was already at it, and within minutes was playing a fish round and out. We had greased our lines thoroughly the night before, and my fly sank and rose as I manoeuvred it across and down in the smoother water. As it approached the lip of the glide on my eighth or ninth cast, a trout took, and rather than 'spoil' the water where I would be searching, I eased it over the lip and down into the roughish stream below, where it was soon beached. It was an afternoon well spent, and we took twenty fish between us before the pool went dead. We kept two for ourselves, and gave the cook the rest to dish up as fairly as he could the next day. Early the next morning the general was off. The sergeant major had arranged for the guard to be turned out and they presented arms as he drove off. Long experience in reading the signs, the varying degrees of rigidity

of posture, and the biff they put into the familiar movements, indicated without need of words that he was one they classified as a
'gentleman'. There were only two other orders in the classification:
'O.K.' and 'a bastard'.

Another 'gentleman', in every sense of the word, was Count
d'Entreves, who lived at Entreves, at the edge of the glacier just
beyond Courmayeur. He was an occasional visitor. At that time I
despised the few partisans I had met or heard of while we were in
action. They enjoyed the name, many of them, without the danger
of self-sacrifice which characterised the true partisans. Dark south-
erners, concerned only with escaping the German call-up, far from
their homes, they would live in the wilds, descend periodically on
lonely farms of their own countrymen, and force them to give up
precious food and grain. Sometimes they made free with the
women, and would leave at night with enough wine and food for a
few weeks. Occasionally they would mine a road, a safe enough
thing to do, and a German staff car or truck would be blown up. The
result was that the hostages from the local population, who had to
take turns weekly at the German headquarters, would be shot out of
hand. Entreves was a different kind of 'partisan'. All through the
Italian campaign, escaping British and American prisoners of war
were contacted and eventually found their way to his home, where
they lived in a secret room until a local guide could lead the party, at
great personal risk, over into Switzerland. He was a man of great
erudition and charm, known in Italy as a philosopher, and at
Oxford occupying a professorship of Italian before the war. His two
sons were in the British Navy. His year had been exactly divided by
three eight-week terms at Oxford and the rest at his home at
Entreves. He was a truly anglicised Italian, and I envied his
well-divided life. At twenty I had left Cambridge to serve in the gunners, and six war years later here I was, near the crest of Europe,
with civvy street waiting, as for so many others of my generation,
and I felt I had no roots. After so many years of almost daily moves
as we crept up Italy mile by mile, I had learnt to live in the moment
and to shut off any thought of the future. This present, at least, was
delightful.

It is a year or two later, the war now a thing of the past, and I have
taken the road from Verres in the Aosta valley, miles down from my

army post at Courmayer, and climbed by a twisty road full of hair-pin bends, for about thirty miles to Champoluc at the head of the valley of Ayas. At the last bend a breathtaking spectacle is suddenly revealed – the alps, rocks and glaciers of the Monte Rosa chain. To the left is the Roccia Nera, the Black Rock, with its steep precipice crowned with glacier. To the right are the twin alps Pollux and Castor, and further to the right the Lyskam. Above Champoluc rises a rock pyramid, too steep for glacier, the Testa Grigia, Grey Head. In the years to come I shall stand at its peak, and on my way back down, watch the young eagles taking the remains of my lunch. These presences, no more than a mile or two away, so dazzle the eye when the last bend in the road reveals them, the air so clear, the sun so dazzling, the white so pure, the green so vivid, that for a moment I have to catch my breath.

This is the place where I shall spend the next two months. I have been here before, know the people, have climbed these alps. I have brought a telescope for a man I met herding his goats high up there near the snow line, and feel the absence of Giancarlo, one of the family of local guides. I was with him last year at the Mezzalama refuge, and heard of his death when he attempted the first winter climb of the Roccia Nera. I have brought my fishing tackle and intend to explore the possibility of fishing some of the many little alpine lakes in the hills above Champoluc. I am speaking of the years immediately after the war, before the tourist boom, when Champoluc had only a two-month summer season for a few rich visitors from Turin, and the locals still knew them respectfully as 'I monsieurs'. It was a time before ski-lifts and speculators introduced a winter season and made the village a tourist town, the barrier of the Alps still happily sealing off its boundaries to all but the hardy and dedicated.

The little chain of lakes have only dialect names, most of them never seen by the locals, who are busy with their herds of cows, the women with the milking, making butter, cooking the daily polenta and raising their families. As I climb up the steeps above the village I try to identify the location of the lakes and their names from the advice I have been given – Lago Pinter? Lago Ciarcerio? Lago Suzzun? It is spring, and I go up through glades of emerald green larches, meadows brilliant with the yellows, blues and pinks of an amazing variety of flowers. Two women with wooden clogs have a sheet and are gathering the heads of some of the thousands of big violets that grow here in abundance. They keep them in the airy haylofts, and when winter comes, a handful in a mug of boiling milk makes a heady brew against winter chills.

I climb up for an hour and at last come to a smooth knoll where I stand and look down on a small lake, cupped in a sort of conch Not a sound breaks the stillness. As I climb down to the lake there is a sudden rushing of wings not far from where I stand. A falcon has stooped in a great rush. A small bird flits away among the rocks having escaped by a hair's breadth. I suddenly realise that I am far from alone. It seems there are eyes everywhere.

I stand for a moment, having mounted my rod, and survey the placid surface of the lake. I have no idea how deep it is, but guess that if the slope of the hills around the edge are anything to go by, it may be deep in the middle. Are there trout here? There can be little for them to feed on, and if there are any here, they will surely be small. I take a small piece of bread from my haversack and throw it out. Instantly it is seized and I thrill at the thought that there are fish here. What do they feed on in winter, I wonder, under a foot or two of ice? I tie on a Grey Duster, a conspicuously hackled fly, and cast out across the lake. Two seconds later it is seized, and a small, snub-nosed troutlet is brought in, fighting vigorously. It darts away as I release it. I wonder what the next cast will bring. I cast across to another part of the lake, and my fly is again taken within a second. Another of the same size. A dozen casts, and a dozen quarter-pounders are taken and released. The sun is strong, the air like wine, and I am intoxicated with this exploration of the unknown. Time now to try something different? I tie on a caddis, apply a small shot, and cast out towards the middle. I count to ten, then move the fly very slowly. I have moved it a yard or two inch by inch, when the rod bends and I am into something a little heavier than the others. I have a fine two-pound leader, so care is essential. I bring it in, and he proves to be a half-pound monster. This is all better than I expected in this solitary lake. I return the fish, and guess that he is older than his size would normally indicate. I light a pipe and look around at the lonely beauty unfolding in all directions.

There is a faint squeaking from some rocks nearby and I learn

later that there are marmots here. The hunter (appropriately his sur-
name is Chasseur) who lives in Champoluc tells me he takes them
in autumn when they are fat with feeding up for winter, and they
taste like fatty pork when roasted. This one at least goes uncaught,
unless the falcon spots him. At this season, when the snow has
begun to uncover the ground, the falcons are active, as I have seen.

I move round the lake. This time I bait a bare hook with one of the
grubs I find under a sliver of rock, apply a shot, and cast out, letting
it sink for a few seconds. With fifteen feet of fine leader I am sure it
will go well down, away from the slight disturbance of the floating
line. A few slow pulls and the grub is taken. I play the fish and bring
it in. Another little half-pounder. There must be plenty of fish here,
but small, through lack of food. I calculate that the smaller fish are
in competition with the slightly larger ones, and are exiled to the
top, while the others feed lower. Probably there are few trout here
above the half-pound mark, and I decide to move across to one of
the other lakes, if I can find it. This has been a thrilling interlude. I
shall have to convince my hosts that I have taken more than a dozen
fish. To them the proof of the pudding is in the eating, and they will
wonder why I have returned all these delicacies to whence they
came. To my mind they have enough to contend with in their fight
for survival without having to cope with the depredations of some
upstart from England.

I move off in the direction of the next lake, which may be difficult to find. These lakes hide themselves well, and they appear suddenly, only when they are reached after much climbing and
scrambling. I am lucky. After an hour of walking, viewing and circling it is suddenly revealed, larger than the others, cupped in surrounding hillocks. The sun is now hot and the rocks as I scramble
down to the water are warm to the touch. I reassemble the rod and
attach the grey duster, and cast. As before, the fly is taken instantly,
but I draw in only a fingerling. I cast again with the same result.
Another cast and another three-inch minnow. Are they all this size
here, I wonder. I search my bag for the quill minnow and attach it to
my leader. I know I cannot cast it like a fly, but I can surely get it out
across the lake if I try. I pull off the necessary yards of line and walk
back with the minnow far enough to extend the line. I lay the
minnow on a piece of flat rock and return to my rod. A quick,

smooth pull and the quill minnow falls out into the lake. I retrieve with gentle pulls. A couple of yards and the minnow is taken. The rod bends, and I am into a heavier fish than any of the others. I play him carefully and beach him in the shale that slopes gently into the water at my feet. He is a good three-quarters of a pound, a beautiful fish, and I note the prognathous effect in his lower jaw. As I unhook him and return him I conclude that he makes his living mostly by feeding on the kind of tiny fish I have already taken. I make a mental note to bring my spinning rod the next time I visit this lake. My quill minnow has only a single tail hook. It would not be possible to return a fish hooked on a treble without damage.

I repeat my ritual of casting, this time at a different angle. I have replaced my leader with one of three-pounds breaking strain, and hope that I will not lose the only quill minnow I have with me. At a distance I can see the little quill revolving, sinking and rising as I retrieve with brief pauses. Bang! It is taken suddenly and I am broken. I regret the loss of my quill minnow, but 'pazienza!' as they say here. I shall try now with fly again, but this time a long-shank polystickle, the nearest I can find to a small minnow. I use it in England in the edges of lakes when the trout are minnowing. I cast far out along the edge of the lake and bring the fly slowly back. The next casts bring no results. I try the other side and am in luck. The fly is taken strongly and I am soon landing another trout only a little smaller than the one I took. In the course of the next hour I take another brace of decent fish, all returned, and decide that it is time to find my way back. An hour later, I reach Crest, a tiny hamlet perched on a ledge directly above Champoluc, looking down the valley where the river, diminished by distance, resembles a silver ribbon twisting its way among the feet of the sleepy descending hills. I am quiet as I pass the rock shelf where the houses stand and am invited in. It is said to be the highest hamlet in Europe. The sun still bakes the yard-thick walls and balconies and shines level into the interiors, all wood-lined for warmth. At this height the sun still beats there long after it has left the houses in the valley below. As I sit on the pine settle, the smell of pine logs burning in the stove fills the air, and the sunlight enters my corner of the room. I gratefully accept the coffee which has been milled, and brewed in the 'Napoletano', not to mention the glass of grappa to follow. What a way to end a day of searching for trout in alpine lakes.

The river which flows through Champoluc is the Evancon. It begins a mile or two beyond, where the valley of Ayas is closed by the barrier of the Monte Rosa chain. It trickles from the melting glacier at Pian di Vera, quickly becomes a snowy torrent, and races through Champoluc, past Antagnod, and leaps down the thirty miles of steep descent to the main Aosta valley. Here it joins the Dora, still known locally as the Doire, the river I fished so happily with the visiting general a year or two ago.

The morning is bright and all is a-dazzle. Wooden clogs cackle on the cobbles as the women go to and fro, one leading a pet cow known as Bianca, which nuzzles her affectionately as she pauses to chat in the local patois with a neighbour. Flowers seem to shout for joy in the pure alpine air. Outside the Albergo Favre they are filling wine flasks from the large butt of Barbera. I pause to sample an offered glass, then I am on my way. I have the spinning rod and a few quill minnows and am off to a place a mile or two downstream where for a few hundred yards the river enters a broad, calm reach. I have noted this many times on my journeyings up and down the valley here in army days, and I intend to explore its possibilities. I follow the riverside road out of the village. Above, on my right, perched up a quarter of a mile away and overlooking the valley is a gracious rustic house with thick, sloped walls, a deep overhang of roof, and open loggia – the Villa D'Orsa, the Bear Villa. In the eighteenth century, when the road where I now walk was a narrow footway, the local priest was returning to the village one winter dusk. Snow was piled deep on either side of the track. Suddenly he was confronted by a bear. Extreme hunger must have brought it down from the wilds above the village. It reared before him, its jaws gaping. In desperation the priest (a tough customer according to the village records) grabbed his cap and rammed it down the animal's throat, choking it to death. One of its paws, complete with talons and fur, is now in one of the church coffers. The other was nailed on one of the timbers of the villa. I have seen it often as I have passed by. The absence of humidity in the air at this altitude has preserved it entire. On a panel of the outside wall a local artist of the time depicted the scene – the upreared bear, the priest thrusting his cap down the bear's throat.

I arrive at the place where the ground levels for a few hundred yards, and the river for once runs calm and unhurried. Who knows?

Are there trout here, or am I on a vain quest? We shall see, though it occurs to me that even though I make no contact, that will be no proof of the absence of trout. I move over to a likely spot and assemble my rod. I light a pipe with the local tobacco – a dry crusty mixture which when smoked in England is strong and acrid. Here, at this altitude and in this dry air it has a wonderful aroma. As I attach the quill minnow I note that though the water runs smoother over here, it still has the colour of melting snow as when I fished the Doire. The slopes above me are blue with pools of gentians among a mass of yellow flowers, which cover the hillsides to right and left. On the rocks beside me I recognise saxifrage, which grew in the rockery at home, and a few of what are called 'botton d'oro' – golden buttons, a full, bulbous, yellow flower. The large, deep-toned bells attached to collars round the necks of the cows in the pastures above and around me maintain a continuous jangle which mingles with the sounds of the river.

I throw the quill minnow I made yesterday from the quills and flights in my kit, first along the edges of the river, downstream on either side. Against this current any other spinner would make too much commotion. The quill rises and falls, light and gentle as a feather. No takes. I try again, this time letting out slack to allow the minnow to sink. Still no sign of life. I cast across and bring the spinner down and around. Nothing. I try again and again, letting the spinner sink and rise, each time going a little deeper. Still no sign of a take. Are there trout here? If so they show no interest in my quill minnow, whose reputation is at stake. I lay the rod down and climb up a few yards above the river. The Stour above Canterbury, where I shall live in a few years' time, will provide the same problems, in a similar contour of the river. I shall learn the solution from the lesson to be learnt today. The place where I have cast appears from where I now stand to have an even bend. A little downstream the angle of gravel at the edges indicates a deeper scooping of the riverbed. Perhaps if there are trout they are lying below the current in deeper water. No trout expends energy in a strong current if there is food to be had in calmer regions. I am only guessing, but wet-fly-fishing in the Yorkshire dales has suggested that when the fish are not 'up', the flies all too often sweep over them. A fly trotted downstream with the current will sink to where they are, and a strike when the fly might have reached a likely lie has often resulted in a take. I move downstream and cast upstream and across. The minnow sinks as it floats down, and when it has gone far enough not to 'spoil' the nearer water where a fish may be lying I begin the retrieve. Instantly it is taken. I play it upstream to avoid disturbing the water down-stream, and soon have a trout of over three-quarters of a pound safely beached. It is like those in the Doire in the main valley, the colour of melting snow. The water is ice-cold and my fingers are numb. Satisfaction; that rare feeling of triumph and self-congratula-tion which all anglers feel when they have tackled unknown water and found their own way of taking the elusive quarry. I slide the trout back, dry my hands and warm them for a moment on the rock where I am kneeling. In my pocket is a flask of grappa and some lumps of sugar. The guides here never, like the tourists in future years, load their stomachs with heavy food. A lump of sugar, soaked in grappa every so often is all they require to sustain them in a long climb to a refuge and back down again before taking up another group. But I am not a guide on a long climb, so I have in my sack a hunk of the bread that they bake here and a large piece of fontina, the local cheese, together with a bottle of wine from one of the butts in the cellar where I am staying.

The sun is now hot, but up here the heat is dry and never sultry. It bakes but never stews. When it thunders, the effect is awe-inspir-ing, echoing and re-echoing. The lightning strikes in places where there are metal deposits, and can be seen hitting at the rocks. When the rain comes it is a brief downpour, and within an hour the clouds are grouping like puffballs and exhaling again in clear blue skies. On such occasions, higher up in the white places, it snows. When it actually rains on the glaciers woe-betide. The waterfalls and streams become swollen, the wooden bridges are swept away, and when the flood subsides huge boulders can be seen where none were before in the riverside pastures.

I repeat my cast, in the same place, and again my minnow is taken and a trout of the same size comes to the side and is released. As I dry my hands I am aware of a strange lack of background sounds and I realise that the cowbells have ceased their jangle – up here, where the grass is so rich, they are allowed to feed for no more than an hour twice a day. More than that makes them swell, and the cowherd has to hole them to let out the gas. My own inner man reminds me that I am hungry, so I decide to get rough with the bread and fontina. I wander a few yards upstream and sit among the mass of yellow flowers. Thyme grows in all the nooks and crannies and gives off an intoxicating scent as I crush the leaves. As I munch at my bread and cheese I am the privileged witness to a strange sequence of events. A brown squirrel with a young one clasped to its back has entered the river upstream and is crossing, carried down about forty yards by the current. It scrambles out and disappears into some trees. I am finishing my meal and sipping the wine ten minutes later when it appears again, entering the water in the same place, again with a young one on its back. It scrambles out in the same place and disappears. As I return to my fishing I ponder on all this. They say squirrels change their nests when they become lousy. This one must have crossed the river, deposited the offspring, returned upstream to cross and been carried down and across to the same place to join the other. I have since wished I had waited to see if there were other trips made by this gallant parent. But trout were still tempting me and I returned to my pursuits, intrigued and eager as ever.

The afternoon sun shines hot, though the icy water cools the air at the edge of the river. At night, up at Champoluc where the torrent runs boisterously past the bordering chalets, and the 'Moulin' where we drink the local Barbera, it is unwise to leave the warmth of the stove unprepared for the sudden icy air of the river. Here, though, I have shed my jacket and am moving down to the next and last likely place for a cast or two. There the lagoon ends, and the river creams past a pile of high rocks where it bends and dives into a waving, surging torrent once more. For a small space near the rocks the water is in shadow, and it is here that I guess a fish or two may be lying in the slack of the current. I take my rod (the one mentioned in the first chapter, which has the pliable tip section of some plastic compound) and move into position. This is the ever-exciting, ever-special moment, when the unknown is about to become known, when a new place, in a river I have never explored, is about to be tested. I hope for the best, but contemplate no worst. To be here, in this special place, in this dancing light at this hour of the day, the alpine sun at its zenith is reward enough. I think of May

morning on the river at home in England, and of those happy, fruit-
less days spent float fishing by the Avon with my brother, and sigh
as I swing the quill minnow slightly up and across, pause for it to
sink, then... Almost before I snap the end-line reel to the retrieve it
is taken, and the trout lunges towards me, then back and down, hec-
tically seeking its freedom. When I bring it in, still fighting, and ease
it over the shale to release it, I calculate that it must be about a
pound and a quarter in weight, long, lean and hungry, and lively
through its fight to survive in these snowy waters. Off it shoots like a
homing arrow. I dry my hands, take off the quill minnow, break my
rod, sling my jacket and bag over my shoulder and prepare to
depart. I wish for no anticlimax in this musical place, on this first
fragrant visit to the Evancon. This is the time to go. I shall come here
again. But next time the mystery of the unknown will have vanished.

10

Cottage Pie

The brook where I have spent countless happy hours challenging the game little trout there, runs for miles through the meadows and valleys of Shropshire to join the Teme near Bucknell. The myriad pleasures are varied, special, and impossible to describe. But bear with me and I shall take you, an unseen presence on my left (all anglers know why observers must stay like shadows, always on the left) for a sortie or two up the brook.

It is early evening in midsummer. We have driven out from home, skirted Ludlow, crossed the hills and descended into Leintwardine. We have paused (of course) to hang over the bridge. The water runs clear and full, streaked by outcrops of flowering cresses. Here and there we can spot the rings of rising trout. The stone of the bridge is warm to the touch, and the river surfs under its low, graceful arches. We leave this sylvan scene, heartened by such appetisers, and wind our way onwards by roads that imitate the river in its curves and eddies. Beyond Brampton Bryan with its familiar yew hedge bordering the road, and then off towards Bucknell we flow. Ten minutes later we are weaving through a veritable Arcadia of meadows and spinneys, over graceful little stone bridges, and at last we pull in by a farm gate. We have arrived. The dross of the week's labours has fallen away from us. We go through the gate, enter the cottage porch, and with a large key open the door. That strange, indefinable smell exhales as we enter and proceed to unload. On a shelf in the porch as we go in and out, a nestful of young open beaks indicates that in the week or two of our absence the swallows have taken advantage of the situation. Within an hour or two of our arrival the parents are busy filling the gaping mouths whenever the porch is unoccupied by human bodies. Kate now takes charge. We have donned our country garb. I light the fire, remembering not to bang head my head on the huge black beam running across the chimney breast. As I return from the shed with a load of long wedges of wood she hands me a mug of tea. In the woods which clothe the little hills and valleys opposite the cottage, the Forestry Commission has cleared wide pathways for their logging. Here and there are huge piles of wood wedges, the leavings of their work. At intervals we have harvested these, filling the boot of the car with this odorous provender. It is stacked in the shed, all ready for occasions such as this.

The fire is already blazing and I am reaching down my rod from one of the beams. Out I go over the stile and down to the brook not 20 yards from the cottage. I walk down the meadow to the 'limit' where a thick outcrop of alders hides the brook from view. A good quarter of a mile of the brook awaits me upstream of open meadow, quick ripples, glides, then a bend where the brook broadens, edged by a spinney and a rock wall; a place where it divides and leaves a little island of cobbles where we sometimes light a fire at dusk and sprawl at ease, roasting potatoes and listening to the sound of the water as darkness grows. A little upstream, where it passes just below the cottage, there is a deeper stretch where the farmer used to dip the sheep, and here, each year I take and return a trout of just over a pound. A little further and the brook narrows and rushes in a curve, overhung by a steep wall where the farm outbuildings stand (here there are 'sinks' of no more than a few feet, where trout lie and are taken). A bypass of a couple of hundred yards to avoid the farm takes us to an open, brimming reach with a plank bridge, under which is a favourite lie. Still further upstream the brook enters a glen with steep sides where even by day there is a mysterious gloom, and the brook stumbles round large boulders to reach a wooden barrier which forms the limit of my fishing. Such is the prospect awaiting us this evening. To fish it all (I know from experience) will take a whole day, for I like to comb every inch. This evening we shall have time to sample only a few choice places before we hear a call from the cottage that the meal is ready.

I attach a small black gnat. In the evening I always fish dry. By day, according to how I feel, I fish wet, line out of the water, the fly dancing across and just under the surface, or 'trotted' to explore the various 'sinks'. There is no need to oil the fly. It travels no more than four or five feet with each cast, and I keep it dry with a few quick false casts. I move forward to a well-known point where a large boulder in a small bay leaves slow water below it. Fishing this brook, at favourite known places, always (or almost always) brings results. I flick the fly, line held well above the water, and it lands on a dock leaf just upstream of the boulder. A twitch, and it swims free, glides round the boulder, and is instantly taken – a 'rose-mole' spotted trout of just over half a pound. No need for a net. I am fishing barbless, and in a moment I have released him and he darts away deep under the boulder. I know the ways of these trout. When disturbed, they dart out frantically and always return to their lie. The brook is too full of hazards for them to risk escape up or downstream.

I straighten up. Wood smoke from the fire I lit a while ago is rising from the cottage chimney. My gaze wanders up the brook, and I suddenly realise, as so often before, that what seemed a river reach while I was concentrating on the water ahead, and edging forward a foot at a time, is, in fact, a mere few yards of brook. When I am absorbed in searching every yard of it, kneeling or bent forward, a quarter of a mile of its twists and turns, its runnels and glides and little pools are expanded in my mind to long reaches of river, a veritable Mississippi. Such is the elusive charm of my Mississippi. The black gnat is a little the worse for its brief sojourn in the troutlet's scissors. As I search my wallet I spot a fly I have never had occasion to use. I bought it with others in a market town not far from here. It is unusual in that it is made of plastic and represents a small spent fly, transparent wings flat, the whole thing beautifully made. I tie it to the leader and approach a bend in the brook where the water runs along under a low rock wall. I try a cast or two to ensure that it floats, then throw it out and begin to comb the bend. The current returns it quickly, as usual, and the casting rate is rapid. I lengthen the cast, keeping the rod well up so that as little line as possible is in the water. A trout snatches at it when it is only a couple of yards from my feet. I cast again, to the same spot, and it is taken instantly. I wonder if it is by the same fish, dashing back upstream to where he was lying. Out he comes, a splendid chap of between a half and three quarters of a pound with a snub nose and a dazzling array of rose-moles along his sides. He joins his confrères in the brook and I edge forward a couple of yards.

Beyond the bend is a wide, smooth glide where more caution is required than in the more broken water. I change the spent fly for another black gnat and cast it to the middle of the glide, letting it return almost to my feet before casting again. Experience has shown that a trout will often follow and take the fly just before it reaches the cobbles at the end of the glide. Not this time. I lengthen the cast and the fly floats gently back. A final cast, this time to the extreme edge of the glide where the brook tumbles in at the top of the bend. The fly lands, is wobbled by something below, is twitched again, then it is taken, and the rod bends as the trout dashes to and fro, oars upstream, zigzags to the right and breaks me against a projecting stone. A satisfying encounter. He took the fly, so I deceived him, and he knew how to rid himself of the fly and so he beat me.

A voice calls from the cottage, and Kate's head and shoulders appear beyond the hedge; twenty minutes to go. The sun is gone and dusk is gathering. I move upstream to where the brook runs in a series of deeper 'sinks' under the wall which borders the farm. Here the trout can almost be counted on to provide a regular rise or two. As I approach I can see the familiar rings as a fish rises just downstream of a large boulder. He is coming up regularly, and taking something invisible to me – something small, and perhaps hidden in the surface film. The gnat, offered gently a couple of times, fails to interest him. Hastily I pick a tiny Coch-Y-Bondhu from my wallet, replace the gnat, and tie on the new fly, snip the nylon above the knot, dunk it in the water so that it will ride in the film, and flick it out towards the boulder. There is a swirl, and my tiny beetle disappears. I tighten and hold the rod high to keep his nose up and so prevent him from dashing round the boulder to break me. He proves to be another plump little half-pounder and soon joins his companions back in the brook. I straighten up and climb the bank to the stile opposite the cottage having wound up my line and hooked the fly near the rod butt. I doff my boots in the porch, replace the rod on its beam in the parlour, and having washed my hands, sit down at the table. The little world of the brook out there is replaced by another, equally savoury, equally demanding.

Tomorrow we must go to collect more logs from the clearings in the woods across from us, and call on Mr Adams. Now over ninety, he is 'an outdoor man' in his own words and missing the wife who saw to the indoor side of their lives from the time he returned from the trenches in the First World War. We met him one winter's day when the snow was swirling thick, pushing his bike past the cottage. We pressed him to come in, and he was soon eating a bacon sandwich before a blazing fire. He was delivering the post to the farms and cottages on the hills around us, and was on his way to the house up on the hill behind us where David, the farm's foreman lived. This meant leaving his bike and climbing up through the steep meadows behind us, a demanding mission for a man already approaching his ninetieth year. In his time he must have been a man to be reckoned with, still tall, big frame, his face set in lines of austere determination. As he sat chatting he told us of the time, many years ago, when he had been a 'floater'. This meant keeping the brook clear and running, covering many miles, and at night, sleeping at whatever farm was on his route. It reminded me of the 'canale', high up in the Italian Alps, running from the glacier of the Monte Rosa along the edge of the mountains of Ayas and descending finally to supply the water at San Vincenzo in the main valley. A similar 'floater's job was to keep it running over thirty or forty miles, damming any breakages in places where it bordered precipitous drops. Mr Adams, as he left, looked towards his cottage, the chimney just visible in a chine a few hundred yards away, and said how sad it was to return there, no smoke coming from the chimney now that his wife was no longer alive to greet him on his return.

But this is no place to dwell on the 'lacrimae rerum'. The farmer allows me to fish the river that runs through his land at Skyborry a mile or two away, the stripling Teme. It is full of lively trout, ever ready to sample my offerings if they are offered at the right time and of the kind they are partial to. I have fished this stretch many times, and at all months of the season. The car is left in a bay well off the road, and there is a scramble down over the steep rocks to reach it where it bends at the foot of a well-scoured clifflet. Below is a fine, clean pool. Upstream and below it ripples and glides and rushes over about a mile of easily waded water, the limit at either end marked by a double line of wire running informally between leaning posts. I have never seen anyone else fishing it, and have grown, through a lazy habit of mind, to feel that the river here (like the brook at the cottage) belongs to me, and I would be shocked to meet another figure with a rod in his hands wading my loved water.

Earlier this year, in late March, I am tackling up and surveying the scene. There have been bursts of sun, and a few gusts of wind, but as I prepare to fish a thin flurry of snow begins to curl and whisk about me. As I gaze, the calm run near the bend where I am standing becomes alive with at least three rising fish, all guzzling at large flies floating in the eddies. The March Brown. I eagerly tie on a dry specimen and cast across and up to the rises. It is taken instantly. I play and release the three-quarter pounder and cast again. It has hardly drifted for a yard when it is taken again. I cast four more times, whipping the fly through the air to dry it before each cast, and take four more fish. They are literally guzzling my offering, and all within feet of where I cast before. When the rise ends I try in vain. I tie on a wet silver March Brown and try, but to no effect. Consummatum est. I move to another stretch but see no more rises.

Downstream there is a straight, wavy run, only a foot or so deep over the cobbles. Here, with a wet, silver March Brown I am soon at work again. I cast straight across, mend the line upstream to slow the fly, and comb the water. After about ten casts, moving slowly downstream, the fly enters a less wavy run and is taken vigorously. I ease him upstream so as not to spoil the water below, and soon have him out and returned – another half-pounder. A few casts further down and the process is repeated. The river, as so often, seems to have plenty of taking fish. I sit for a moment, feeling that sense of gentle fulfilment known to all of my kind in similar circumstances. The water wagtail a little down river, perched on a protruding boulder, true to his name is wagging for all he is worth. The sun has emerged and for the last five minutes has lit up the river like a searchlight, the effect enhanced by the deep, ominous slate-blue of a bank of cloud not far away, auguring another snow shower. I move down to a place where the river bends and narrows, then dives into a quiet pool. I shall have a few last casts at the tail where the water shallows and creams over a lip into a boisterous torrent beyond. Here I have often been successful. It is as if the trout see their food about to escape in the faster current as it speeds towards the lip, and decide on a quick dash, lacking in all caution. My fly sails out. I give slack to let it sink, then draw it gently across. As it nears the lip it is seized, and a dazzling little half-pounder is soon being slipped from the hook (I always fish barbless here) at my feet. As I walk back upstream and scramble up the clifflet to the car, I bless this marvellous beat for its responsiveness at almost all months of the season.

One day in early summer is particularly fragrant in memory. We have made an early sortie from the cottage to have breakfast by the river, driven the mile or two over the hills and down again to Skyborry. K sorts out the various requisites we have unloaded from the car and sets up her cuisine under a bank on the cobbles by the river. I walk off with the rod down a dimpling stretch where I am usually lucky and begin casting across, a sparse black spider on the point. Round and down it travels, moving gently with the current. Midstream it is taken, brought to my feet and dispatched. Within half an hour I am making my way back with four plump trout for the pot – or rather the pan. The fire is already ablaze and K has a kettle boiling. I prepare the trout while the bacon fat sizzles in the pan, and the fillets are soon cooking in a row. The sun is warm, the tea is strong, the air is heady with its riverside tang, and the trout are delicious. Idylls such as this are memorable because they are rare and brief. The rest of the day has faded from my memory, but that high point remains, like the brief pool of sunlight seen lighting the hills on a day when the clouds soon roll it all away.

Lower down the Teme is another reach I have fished only once or twice, and remembered for its sylvan charm. I discovered it while exploring the countryside during a week at the cottage. A road leads off the main Knighton road and curves over a stone bridge. From here the river wanders in a series of curves and runs until further upstream it becomes a wide, shallow meander which in the height of summer dries to a trickle, finding its way mostly underground to its fuller course downstream. A word with the owner of The Hall, with its magnificent yew hedges, and I have permission to fish there after Mayfly time. What a thrill it is to explore new water, every bend a discovery, every yard a fresh revelation, instinct with unknown possibilities. A well-known stretch of brook or river, where every yard is known, every angle the scene of a take – such a possession is precious. And yet the call of new waters is strong, but, by definition, brief. Once explored, new water ceases to be new. It has been tested, its advantages and limitations are known, and it must take its place in the long hierarchy of merit order.

Here, my Skyborry approach pays no dividends. The downstream wet fly has no appeal for the trout. Either the pools are too deep, or the runs are too fast. I move upstream and see no rise. It is ten o'clock and the sunlight dapples the riverbed with its amber-tinted pebbles. I tie on a pheasant-tailed nymph, weighted, and begin casting upstream. The nymph sinks and comes quickly back towards me. It is a matter of searching the water. Nothing doing. It is as if a warning had gone out for all trout to be confined to barracks for the day. I remove the nymph and tie on a stone fly creeper. Perhaps it will drift over the cobbles on the bottom and tempt some bolshy fish out of barracks against orders. I throw the fly further upstream to give it time to sink well down before it comes back, and keep the rod well up in order to limit the amount of line on the river. In such clear water, in strong sunlight, the line must have a shadow like a cable on the riverbed. A few casts, and suddenly there is a pause in the returning line and I tighten into a fish. The rod bends and the reel screeches as the trout oars lustily upstream. For a moment the line is slack as it comes towards me and I raise the rod high to take up the slack. Just in time. He's still on - and a good fish by all indications. Down and across and up again he goes until I get his nose up, and he comes to the net. In fast water I always let them go downstream, the net behind them to avoid a shambles. He is over a pound, dazzling in his spotted glory, and I return him gladly to his watery haunts.

I am about to lean against the bank, the water just knee level round my waders, and light a cigarette, when just ahead, in a stretch of slower, smoother water, there is a rise, followed by another and another. One or two small files are coming down. I must guess what will meet the situation. I remove the creeper and search the dry-fly wallet for one of my favourite, all-purpose flies, a Greenwells Glory (affectionately known to my fishing confrères as the G.G.). I tie it on, dunk it in the fly flotant, whisk the rod to and fro to dry it, then out it goes, a yard beyond where I saw the rises. It swims serenely, temptingly. I feel I could eat it myself. It is well past where the rise was seen, and I am almost about to pull it back and cast again when it is taken with a sure surge, and the rod is bending again. The trout must have followed it and decided to take it only a couple of yards from where I am standing. It comes to the net, is freed, still in the water, and I flick the fly to dry it. Just under a pound is my guess.

So it goes on. Up I move, round bends, up pools and runs. Here and there are risers, and all of them respond. When I step out of the water at the top end where the river becomes a wide, shallow rush over the cobbles, a kingfisher skims towards me with a turquoise flash, and I wander back to the car, drugged and happy, thinking of the words of the Italian poet Ungaretti, 'M'illumino d'immenso' – 'I am lit with immensity.'

One of the pleasures of our visits to the cottage is the variety of trout fishing in the brooks and the Teme. At Knighton (I am now writing of the sixties and seventies) I have discovered that the Teme upstream of Knighton is free. I am surprised when I explore it to find nothing to impede my progress. I have peered over the wall across from the old railway station, now a woodyard, and seen the trout lying there in the deeper parts, and felt my fingers twitching. I leave the car just beyond the church by the river, where someone has decided to store thousands of used car tyres. I climb the well-constructed style, with signs 'To Offa's Dyke' and pull my waders up. The river purls invitingly. Along the edges of small boulders grow banks of flowery weed and it is here that a wet fly can provide plenty of sport. Nothing is rising, so I decide to go up to the limit, half a mile away, and fish downstream. Near the bridge is a placid pool, a mile or two below my Skyborry stretch, and there in the shadow, a trout is rising, every ten seconds. I remove my wet fly and tie on a small dark Greenwell, dunk it in flotant, whisk it, and position myself well downstream. The water is smooth and a clumsy cast may disturb the unsuspecting incumbent. The fly lands light as a feather just under the bridge and a yard beyond where the fish is rising. As it drifts past the vital spot, a nose nudges it, and it continues its journey back to me. Another cast with the same result. Experience on the brook has taught me not to change the fly, but to position it in the surface film, not to float it on the surface. I hastily remove the fly, replace it with an identical one, and instead of dunking it in flotant I dunk it in the water to ensure that it will float in the surface film. This done, I crouch low and cast again. Hey presto! It is taken immediately and a lively three-quarter-pounder is soon being slipped from the hook and being returned to the water. I feel pleased with myself.

But anglers must beware of hubris, the overweening self-confidence which led the Greek tragic heroes to tread the red carpet and go to their doom. What succeeds once may not succeed again. How many times has the inexperienced angler been deluded into believing he has found the answer, the sure-fire way to success. On a certain day on the lake, in a dead calm, the sun hot and high, when all others have failed, he has tied on a corixa and been instantly taken. He has cast again and been taken again - and again. He retires with his limit and his key to success. In a flat calm, in hot sun, the corixa is the answer. Alas! In an identical situation, all other anglers failing, he approaches the water swollen with hubris, ties on this secret answer to the situation, and fishes all day in vain. In angling nothing is certain. The trout obey other laws than the ones we credit them with and this, surely, is the essence of the sport-and its charm. The experienced angler must learn not to curse when he has fished for hours in vain, and the young tyro mounts his rod and is into a fish at the first cast.

Swollen with humility I turn and prepare to fish downstream. I tie on a sparsely hackled spider, anoint the leader with sinkant, and begin casting. All the way down, in the hour or two I spend here, I see no one. It is a scene of musical tranquillity. I comb the water, pulling out several small trout from the fast river. The best fish, I discover, are lying in the foot-deep runnels under the flowing weeds. Here they have cover and can spot the food surging past their noses and seize it with the minimum of effort. To take them it is necessary to move away and a little downstream. The fly can then land at the top of the runnel and drift along it without a drag from the current. Accurate casting is called for. An inch or two too far and the fly lands on the weed. After an hour or so the effect is hypnotic, and the world shrinks to the four or five yards of white, flowing weed and dazzling runnel. Almost each run holds trout. Sometimes they are taken, and sometimes I tighten too quickly and they reject the fly. It is enthralling work. By the time I reach the church again I am glutted. I step out of the water, doff my waders at the car, fix the rod and reel to the roof rack, and drive to the High Street where I do the shopping before returning to the cottage through a mile or so of hills and valleys. The world of work seems far away, but I must return to it all too soon. But my "inward eye" will visit these places often during the sweat of labour and in "the burden and heat of the day."

11

When Nothing Goes Right

In paradise we must sometimes expect to meet the serpent among the cresses and sedges of the riverside. In most cases he turns out to be harmless, a legitimate denizen in the haunts where we wander. But there are occasions when all unexpectedly he hisses and strikes.

> "It is the bright day that brings forth the adder
> And that craves wary walking."

Brutus, though not an angler, hits the nail on the head. When we set forth in the bright morning we should always have these warnings in mind. Disaster can strike even on such days. Though the river will not run dry as we approach it, fate may have many a trick up its sleeve. It is as well to remember that enigmatic Roman tomb inscription 'Et in Arcadia ego'. Does the 'I' refer to the one buried there – 'I too, was once in Arcadia'? Or is there also a more sinister meaning – 'I, (death) am here, even in Arcadia'? For present purposes, we can transpose this second 'I' to something less final, something which merely marks this particular day as a "dies non", not to be entered in our blissful records, but remembered as a warning for the future.

After such pour parlers, if lesser things can be compared with greater, let us note these trifles in the scheme of things. Every angler will recognise them as part of his experience and rejoice that he alone has not been chosen for punishment by the serpent. Michael Hordern illustrates this with all honesty, and unintentionally, in a short television programme. He is seen in his den, mumbling joyfully as he ties some flies. He lumbers along to the riverside in his waders, rod in hand. He does a few false casts and his fly is immediately caught up in some trees on the backcast. The angler who views this instantly recognises the reality and honesty of the programme. Away with those in which the experts are seen casting with no such hindrances to rises in ideal waters, strike, play and land their fish. Michael Hordern, disentangling his cast, mumbling and replacing it, is the true wayfaring Christian. It is he who enters our hearts because he has shown us the reality and made us see our fallible selves. This has happened to us. We make mistakes, approach the river full of hubris, and the red carpet trips us. We make mistakes and resolve not to make them again.

I have set off in carefree mood and travelled for an hour to a stretch of river where I look forward to trying out my new, whippy, split-cane rod. (The reader will gather from the mention of "split-cane" that this is an incident from the far-away and long-ago.) I arrive, don my waders, mount my rod, and lo! There is no reel. How on earth did I forget such an important item? The expedition is over. I watch a fish rising upstream and quietly curse, calling myself names I would be offended to hear from anyone else's lips. (How often we look about and thank heaven for the solitude that cannot be dismayed by the profanity that mingles with the river sounds and, happily vanishes away without record!) I drink coffee from the thermos I have remembered to bring, noting all the other items of gear which are now surplus to requirements, then with a longing glance at the river, doff my waders, dismount my rod, and return home with my tail between my legs. The serpent has bitten, "Et in Arcadia", but I have been warned for the future. Forever after, all the necessaries are stored in a fishing bag and checked before departure. I have only to pick it up and sling it in the car boot. In summer the bag is replaced by a fishing waistcoat, or by an American chest bag which can be slung or hitched round the waist. It opens in various sections which remain horizontal, and contains every item for every occasion, together with spring attachments for priest, scissors, hook sharpener, fly drier and so on. I was bitten, and the experience healed me.

Again, a year or two later, I set off in carefree mood. I arrive at the river, open the boot, don my waders, mount the rod, attach the reel, sling the net, hitch on the fishing bag and slam down the boot lid. I check that I have my car keys and suddenly realise that after opening the lid I dropped them in the boot, where they now remain. I can neither open the boot nor enter the car. I am faced with the prospect of two alternatives; to fish in doubtful joy, knowing that I shall have to force my way into the car at the end, or do the reverse. I choose the latter. I break the window on the driver's side, scramble over the back seats, and find the keys. The glory of the day is gone. I decide to renounce the fishing and set off back. For years after I always kept a spare key in my wallet, which always remained on my person, and I never removed the key from the boot lid until it was ready to be closed. In later years all has become easy. A lever near the driver's seat opens the boot. Provided that locking the car door is the last thing to be done, even if the boot lid is slammed down with the keys inside, all I have to do is lift the lever near the driver's seat and the lid springs open – et voilà!

I am young and foolish (though not yet full of tears) and in my early angling days. The river burbles nearby and my fingers tremble as I mount the rod, attach the reel and thread the leader through the rings, laying the rod on the grass, the rod tip resting on a low wall. I attach a fly and as I dunk it in a bottle of flotant and step back I slip, and in recovering step with my full weight on the rod tip. The serpent has struck. The day is dark with doom. The expedition is over. But the lesson, so harshly taught, is never forgotten. Ever after the rod is never laid down, either in threading the leader or in changing the fly. I lean it on a tree or against a fence.

Why should a priest always be kept attached to bag or person by cord or spring retractor? Let us go back to one of those days when nothing goes right. I have landed a good fish, which lies in the net. I take the priest from my pocket and reluctantly despatch the trout (these are early days and a tyro's pride requires that he return home with the evidence). I lay aside the priest and begin to detach the fly, the trout still in the net. It is hooked in the scissors and difficult to remove. I finally succeed, place the trout in a plastic bag, stow it in the fishing bag and pick up the net. The fly has become firmly hooked in the cords of the net and it takes me minutes to remove it. I telescope the handle, hinge the net and reattach it to the clip on my belt. I take up the rod and proceed on my way – minus the priest. Half a mile upstream when I need it again it is no longer there. I return to the place where I last used it and find it again, after much searching. The business which followed its last use ... unhooking the fly, the struggle to detach it from the cords of the net, stowing the trout, replacing the net and hooking the fly to the rod handle had been enough to make me forget the priest somewhere there in the grass. The lesson is learnt. Always keep the priest on a retractable cord. Another lesson learnt from this occasion is worth recording. When a fish is safely landed, lay the net down with the fish tightly enclosed in the mesh. If it is to be dispatched, do the deed, then remove it from the net before detaching the fly. This way there is no risk that the fly will become barb-hooked in the cords of the net.

I am by now an experienced operator on the river. The morning shines. The river sings. It is May, and the hawthorn fly is out in clouds. The air around the bushes is thick with these charming, ungainly morsels. I kneel by the verge and wait for the appearance of one or two on the water. I have one ready on the leader and have dunked it in the water so that it will float half submerged. Experience has taught me that they seem to be taken more readily this way than when fished entirely dry. The day is warm, and I am wearing wellies in place of waders. I light a cigarette, and as I move, a large ragged-looking bird flutters out and becomes hooked on the barbed wire on the opposite bank. The river is narrow here and about waist deep in the middle. The unlucky creature struggles and cannot free itself. It is too painful to watch. A rise a few yards upstream indicates that the hawthorn flies are on the water. No matter. I doff my wellies, trousers and underpants, hitch up my shirt, replace my wellies and begin to wade across. The water is icy-cold and I notice a crop of young nettles adorning the bank above which the bird is struggling. As I grasp the bank and pull myself up, the bird makes a last desperate flutter and is suddenly free and away. I wade back, the water now seeming even colder. I empty my wellies, take off my shirt and make a shift to dry myself down from the waist. My legs smell of water mint and I have been thoroughly stung by the nettles. I replace underpants, trousers and socks and run about in the meadow to warm myself. Half an hour later I don my wellies, still wet inside, and am ready to renew the quest. This has been an unexpected interruption but I have no regrets.

Capricious fate, however, has not yet finished with me. "As flies to wanton boys are we to the gods". The words will come to mind later when I am driving home. Downstream, at the edge, something is moving. A large alder is just below it, so it cannot be fished from downstream up. I attach a small Butcher and cast down to where the water is still moving. Instantly it is taken, or so it seems. I tighten, but nothing happens. It cannot be moved. I walk downstream, thinking I must be hooked in the sedges at the side. I take the leader in my hand and find that I have lassoed a small vole, which lies there in the weeds, inert and dead. The cast must have slipped round its neck, caught the hook, and made a slipknot. The poor creature has been garrotted. I cut off the fly, break the rod and walk slowly back to the car. I have no more heart for fishing on this sunny day.

Once more I am on the river. It is late June and the mayfly is still appearing here and there, and being taken. I am making my way upstream, looking for rises and slowly approaching a place where I can usually count on success... a slow glide under a curve of bank where the trout seem to be always up and about. I take my time, approaching my favourite spot with calm confidence. The day is young and still full of infinite possibility. As I stand, the river rumpling musically round my waders, Croesus himself cannot have felt himself richer than I at this moment. The village clock, half a mile away among the trees, begins to chime the three-quarters. Alas! "Et in Arcadia ego," he is here, even in this Eden. A figure, bedizened like a Christmas tree, his hat stuck all over with enormous flies of every hue, "innumerable of stains and splendid dyes", jolts me out of my meditations. He is walking fast, almost running. His fishing waistcoat is new and garnished with every type of attachment. He sees me, gives no greeting, and scuds off. He must be a new member, otherwise this would have been the occasion of a friendly pause in operations, an exchange of titbits of information, and prelude to his final departure to a point at least half a mile upstream. Not so with this deus ex machina who has appeared, it seems, not to save the situation but to produce a dramatic peripeteia, a sudden reversal of fortune in the manner of Greek tragedy. To my surprise I see him halt and begin thrashing the water not twenty yards ahead of where I stand, and in the very place I have been approaching with sure gloating expectancy. No fly angler of any experience could possibly commit such a flagrant breach of protocol. You see an angler moving upstream and concede at least a quarter of a mile ahead to be his. He has stated his claim by being there, and his water must not be encroached on. What is to be done? Mary Killen would surely provide an answer, but this is no time to be posting letters to the agony aunts of protocol. I continue casting, hoping that the intruder will vanish as suddenly as he appeared. But the sun of the morning is now a harsh glare, and my favourite glide is being raped by some tyro from outer space. Shall I confront him and deliver a rocket as in army days? Shall I give him a polite lecture on the do's and don'ts of angling etiquette? Or shall I approach, give him a glare of "austere regard", Malvolio-like, and begin to fish just twenty yards ahead of him? Or shall I refrain, and when I sign off at the box, leave a quiet comment in the relevant space? I do none of these things. Why commit some pompous absurdity? He is probably quite unaware of having given any cause for complaint. I step out of the water, hitch my fly to the rod and amble slowly past to renew my delicious pursuits a good half-mile from where he stands threshing the water, as I note with pleasure, to no effect. The serpent has struck, but probably unintentionally, and the antidote lies here before me in the guise of a trout rising just ahead within easy casting distance.

12

A Winter Pike

In the spring, before the season opens and the river receives its first stocking of trout, the river authority comes to electro-fish certain beats. A small, flat-bottomed boat is brought on a trailer and placed in the water. The slow current drifts it downstream while a man aft guides the boat with a paddle and one in the bows searches the water with an instrument carrying an electric current. A few members of the club attend the ceremony, to help, or out of curiosity and interest. As stunned fish rise to the surface they are netted. The trout are returned to the water behind the boat, while coarse fish are taken and placed in containers on board the Land Rover. These will be taken by members of the river authority and transferred to the waters of local coarse fisheries. Every year forty or fifty pike are taken from one beat alone. In return for the coarse fish the river authority gives the club a few hundred small trout and their services in the electro-fishing. The whole ceremony is broken by an interval in the village pub where drinks and sandwiches for the river authority personnel are at the club's expense. The whole arrangement is a pleasant one for all concerned. No one loses ... not even the fish.

How exciting it is on a fine day in March, the season about to open, to follow the slow drift of the boat and be granted a miraculous viewing of the contents of a favourite beat. Here and there a few whoppers float up, some stretches revealing abundance of the finny tribe, others strangely uninhabited. We, mere interested spectator-helpers, note all this as we ruminate on the days to come when we shall be here with our rods in earnest

Before all this, in those lean months of mixed weather before the season opens, there is little to do but lie fallow and sample those pre-prandial appetisers noted in the first chapter. The river and surrounding meadows are often flooded. On fine days it is strange to walk along familiar reaches and find them hard to recognise without their summer finery. Occasionally, armed with saw and slasher, I seek out my favourite haunts and clear dead vegetation, remove offending branches or drag out submerged logs carried down by winter floods. But there remains another consolation. When the river has calmed down and the weather invites, it is possible to set out armed with spinning rod and end-line reel to search for pike before the electro-fishing does the job for us in earnest.

I set off to the river in high spirits, glad to be in action again, though with different tackle and with deadlier intentions. I have arranged my spinning attachments in their broad plastic case, which now hangs in the bag at my shoulder. It contains artificial dead bait, spoons, vibros, devons, tobies, spare swivels and steel traces. In my pocket are pliers and a priest (duly attached!) and a net hangs from a ring at my side. My spinning rod is the one already described in these pages and just the right length for this little river. This is a trip into the unknown. The river will be difficult to spin without frequent snagging. The pike are there in mid-March but are they here now? And where do they come from? Some say from the Severn, a mile or two away, but the intervening obstacles seem to preclude this as a possibility. The beat beyond the village seems pike-free, so the likelihood is that the creek which joins the river on this side of the river is the route they take

I cross the meadow to the river and make for a bend where it runs a little deeper and may have scoured a hole where pike could lie. I mount the rod and confront the problem of what to attach to the trace. Spinners, vibros and tobies may attract the odd trout so I reject them and plump for the large, metal dead-bait in the hope that no trout will attempt such a meal. I throw out the bait, the guard-arm snaps down, and I begin to manoeuvre it through the water. I let it submerge, then tighten in a series of movements which I hope will help it to resemble an ailing fish struggling to survive. In it comes and I cast again, bringing the bait out of the current into the back eddies. On the third cast I am about to seek another spot, the bait dangling for a moment in the water under the bank where I stand, when at the very moment I pull it out, it is seized, bending the rod as it is rushed away into midstream. There follow a series of quick dashes for which I have slackened the brake. How different from the behaviour of a hooked trout with its variety of curving manoeuvres. When the fish seems to have exhausted some of its initial efforts I tighten the brake, bring him to the net, scoop him out and dispatch him, regretting that there is no waiting tank for his transfer to other waters. He weighs seven pounds, and the river, from the trouts' point of view, is well rid of him. Was he waiting there under the bank at my feet all the while I was casting into the current, or did my bait attract him to pursue it from out in the stream to where it was seized at the edge? I shall never know.

I pause, excited, surprised, and rather pleased to have taken the current when it served and not lost my ventures. I came with no positive expectations, only hope. This was an excuse for going to the river in the close season for trout with a rod in my hand. I am amply rewarded. The day is a success whatever is to follow.

I move downstream and explore every hole, angle and crevice at the next bend without success. Four or five new places are tried with no sign of a response from Mr Luce. Now I come to a deep, slightly sinister, oily-smooth run where over the years I have never seen a trout rise. Here, because of the current, I try a different approach. I drop in the bait at my feet and let it submerge. I bring it up, let it drift, then retrieve again, very slowly. This is surely a tempting offering if only there is a pike to see it. I have heard a colleague say of his nicely cocked grey duster drifting near a rise on one of our lakes, "I could eat it myself!" Sure enough, a few yards downstream as I raise the bait, the rod bends and I seem to be snagged. As I tighten and move the rod-tip I realise that something, probably a pike, is tugging violently. The snag is suddenly gone and the bait is being rushed downstream. The brake is slackened, and after a series of straight rushes I bring the fish to the net, land and dispatch him. Eight pounds. Pondering on this encounter I come to the conclusion that my bait did indeed snag on some weeds and the pike must have seen it, begun worrying it, and freed it only to meet his own doom.

All this is better than I expected. The pike are here, and in spite of weeds and the difficulty of managing the bait in this bendy, uneven stretch of river, my efforts have been reasonably rewarded. I move on, trying likely places without success. The day is still and it is pleasant to renew my acquaintance with the river, albeit in its winter dishabille, and with the charms of spinning. I remember how, years ago on the Kentish Stour, on a wide reach downstream of Fordwich, a long cast with a tiny articulated plug could place it in a shallow, dimpling run where it behaved like a tiny acrobat and attracted the trout like magic. Different times, different places, different approaches! I arrive at a place where the river does a right-angled bend and is perhaps at its deepest, the current appearing to slow because of the deeper water. Just below here, in a run about thirty yards downstream three seasons ago I took six fish in quick succession, two of them dace of over the three-quarter-pound mark, the rest plump brownies, all returned. Today the slow glide

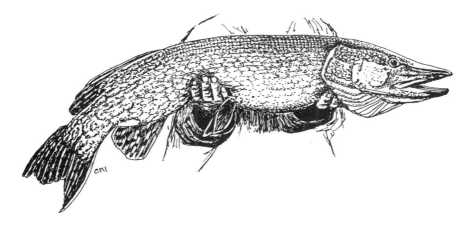

looks strangely hostile, the water impenetrable in its dead season mood. I throw out the bait and begin the now familiar manoeuvre. It is taken immediately. The pike rushes away and I am broken. I wind in. The bait and trace are gone The nylon must have parted where it joined the top swivel. I sigh regretfully, but without annoyance. This is not one of those occasions on which to treat the air and surrounding trees to a volley of winged words. Success has preceded failure. My bait was taken and I accept the inevitable.

A few weeks later there is to be an interesting sequel to this encounter. I am out to "help" with the electro-fishing of this beat. The day is sunny, the trout season about to open, and there is a happy mood among the four or five members here to "help". We have not met since last season, and there is much chatting and information-giving. I have mentioned the above encounter, the lost bait and trace. Suddenly a pike drifts up stunned as the river is swept. It is netted, and as it is taken to the tank on the truck the river authority man bends down and gives me a shout. He is holding up my bait and trace, which he has just removed from the pike's jaws. I rejoice, not so much as having it back, but in the thought that having made such a lucky escape from my priest, this pike will live to swim in other waters. To live and let live is my own recipe for the pleasantest angling.

But I am still here by the river in mid-February, my dead bait gone, and pondering what to do. I select a small spoon from the box, snip off two of the hooks from the treble with my pliers, attach swivels and trace, and renew my efforts. Two casts later a little further down the glide and the spoon is taken. There is no familiar rush but an even more familiar plunging and swerving to indicate that I am into a trout. With this tackle there will be no gentle playing as with a three-pound nylon leader. I bring it to the net and lift it to the bank – a two-pound rainbow a-dazzle with its glorious over-wintered finery. I ease the hook out and hold it in the water. It hangs for a moment, gills moving, then streaks away. I congratulate myself on having removed the two hooks from the treble, which made its release possible. I hook up the spoon, light a cigarette and begin my trudge across the meadow and up the slope to the car. There are always too many over-wintered trout in the river to risk continuing my pursuit of pike without the large, artificial dead-bait. The next time I fish here will be with fly-rod and three-pound leader. The river will be wearing its emerald green dress and will keep its tryst with me as sure as anything can be sure. Perhaps then I shall renew my brief acquaintance with the rainbow, and again return him to his rightful haunts.

13

Casting a Shadow

We had taken the single track railway from Ross to Symonds Yat and walked the riverside path by the salmon pools to Monmouth. On· the way we had picked blackberries as large as plums. I was ten years old. There were cherry plums in the hedges and wild strawberries on the shady banks. I had seen my first kingfisher. At that time a great variety of butterflies haunted the Wye in that loveliest of sequestered reaches. I had seen in the hot sunlight the sudden flash of a salmon falling back in the water and had drunk in the mystery and silence. Those primal moments in that river's powerful presence have always re-established themselves on subsequent visits over the years with their unfailing magic.

Arrived at Monmouth, sleepy in those days, ripe with the smell of cider, paraffin lamps and fatty buns known as " lardy busters", we bought plums from the waspy stalls and had tea at a table crowned with a bowl of sweet peas. It was after all this that I saw the angler who made me realise that sooner or later I must have a rod like his, stand in a river like him and flick the line back and forth with the same leisurely mastery. I saw him from the Monnow bridge, knee-deep in the river, hat tilted over his eyes, the line going out in long, graceful arcs with such beauty of movement that it held me spellbound. From that moment I knew that to fish in this way, whatever it was, was what I wanted to do more than anything else. I saw the rod bend, a commotion in the water, and a fish came to his net. I saw him unhook it, tap it, put it in his bag, relight his pipe and resume casting a few yards downstream with godlike unconcern. It is a memory vignette that has remained with me ever since, and has coloured, I suppose, all my images of rivers, rods and angling.

Some years ago there was a television series on the 1914-1918 war. The Imperial War Museum produced from its archives the kind of news film that made the contrived fictions of most war films seem spurious by comparison. Each episode was introduced by a still depicting a tin-hatted Tommy leaning against the parapet of a trench, a cigarette between his lips. The expression on his face somehow embodied all the emptiness of that spiritual and physical no-man's-land. The figure had a Rembrandtesque grandeur and was unforgettable. Those two figures, the man knee-deep in the Monnow, and the one overshadowed by the parapet of a trench, symbolise for me the two polarities of human experience.

It was years before I found myself at last with my own fly-rod knee-deep in the Skirfair, a tributary of the Wharfe beyond Grassington.. I was twenty-seven. Six and a half years in another war had made me a late starter. But the image of the happy man knee-deep in the Monnow long ago remained, and remains with me.

14

Coarse Fishing on the Wye

Not so far away from the Monnow bridge mentioned already in these pages is another, which for me spans more than its river, the Wye. It is the suspension bridge at Foy, opposite Hole-in-the-Wall farm, The road from Ross winds through Brampton Abbots where my father was born and ends four miles on at the farm. If you open gates and continue past How Caple Court and on to Fownhope they will tell you of the thirty-nine pound salmon taken that morning from the river nearby. But stop with me at the suspension bridge in 1936 and admire the "elm stick" by the roadside, a huge tree trunk which Jim, the farmer, tells me has been there as long as he can remember. This was once a ford in Roman times and the river is shallow for the Wye in this spot, even today. The charm of the bridge is that it is very low-slung, not more than a yard or two above the water. An added charm is that because the sides consist only of steel cables there is no need to stretch for a view of the river or compress the body against a parapet. There is the further pleasure of a slight swaying and a feeling of dangling, and as you proceed to the centre, a feeling of being in perfect eye contact with every inch of the river below. Upstream or downstream, according to the light, there is perfect visibility. All this fabulous river's secrets are revealed to the eye of the dedicated searcher on the bridge. Add to this the knowledge that (eager novitiate from the northern Fylde that I am) the Wye harbours large trout, vast pike, enormous salmon, and your eye will be too busy peering into the streamers of weed which "go to and fro, lackeying the varying tide" to notice, just across the cornfield on the other side, the squat little church of Foy. Nor will you be troubled by the graves under its yews and the roll of honour inside commemorating the boys of the village lost in the First World War (the second one is yet to come). Fanny, who is Jim's mother-in-law, has a dresser in the parlour of the farm decked with badges, photographs, buttons and medals of her ten sons, all killed in the war. Jim's wife, Betty, is the sole surviving offspring. Yet here Fanny is, after all those telegrams, with a machete in her hand (which she calls "the 'acker") telling us where we can fish.

We have come down to stay with them on the farm for a fortnight. Fanny is my father's fifth cousin, I am told. There are seven of us: my two elder sisters, my brother, my two schoolfriends and my younger sister's fiancé. We have had ham and eggs in the Tabard in Hereford, looked down the little snickets between old houses and shops to garden vistas bright with flowers and sniffed the haunting tang of cider at the doors of half-timbered inns. My sisters are keen sketchers and wild flower identifiers and have bought sketchpads to be inscribed while we others fish. At Ross we have bought fishing licences and have walked the four miles along the twisting road to the farm at Foy in the heat of the August afternoon. We have had tea in the little parlour off the farm kitchen, sluiced ourselves at the pump (the girls have other arrangements in a bedroom away in the upper reaches of the farm), changed our clothes and made a tour of the garden and the farm, noting the cider press and the cider mill and the great tuns of cider down in the cellar (which Jim assures us we shall sample tonight). At last we move off to inspect the places down the steep, fifteen-foot banks downstream which Fanny has pointed out with the "acker".

There is the musky smell of the Wye vegetation, a sweetish river smell, and the impressive gurgle of the water, now deep and fearsome after the even, shallower water under the bridge. The whole body of the river seems to be moving, and we remember tales of the crew of a "four" of Monmouth Grammar School, all drowned when they upset, and of the powerful undertow which accounted for many a bather in the smiling horseshoe bend at Ross – tales of the river's murky past from my father's boyhood memories. We complete our tour and return with dusk closing in, a white mist enshrouding Wye's wide-bordering meadows. Bullocks eyeing us as they group round a feeding trough, and about half a dozen lights from the paraffin lamps in half a dozen cottages, widely dispersed, are the only visible signs of life in all the darkling valley stretching out before us. We wend back to the farm, subdued, excited, a little apprehensive. The spell of the Wye is on us. Tomorrow we shall be up at four. We can hardly wait.

In the farm kitchen the "girls", as my sisters are always referred to, are already full of plans for sketching as we sit down with Jim and Betty at the big table. Partridge, pheasant, chicken, ham from the beams, with the bristles still attached, all figure in the menu over the fourteen never-to-be-forgotten days of our stay. Jim, who drinks a whole keg of cider in a morning before coming in to breakfast (he is always up and out by four o'clock) confines himself to Betty's crusty bread, cheese, and onion, and more cider. Every ten minutes the jugs are taken down to the cellar and refilled. Jim drinks only from a cow's horn. His is the paler cider, too acid for us. We drink the sweet cider from another barrel. His cellar is open to all. One evening, after his once-a-week shave, he is taking us out to show us off to some of his friends. (How can he be proud of us? With his bronzed face, benevolent smile and deep-voiced Herefordshire cadences he has become what in these days would be called a role model.) As we pass the hedge slasher plying his way homeward past the farm, parched after his hot day's labours, Jim pauses and hands him some keys. We ask, and he tells us they are the keys to the cellar where, he tells us, the hedge slasher will drink half a gallon of cider before walking the four miles to where he lives, "up

arranged permission for us to fish below the bridge but knows nothing about the gentle art. He tells us of the days when, as a lad, he saw
some labourers dynamite the stretch above the bridge and collect
the salmon lower down, standing strung out above the ford to net
them as they drifted by. He also tells us to watch out for adders on
the banks. Adders, he claims, sometimes bite and kill salmon. We
make a note to wear wellies tomorrow.

We are up at four. Jim is already off, and we move across the
bridge in the quiet before dawn. There is that "unforgettable,
unforgotten" river smell and the valley seems to be holding its
breath. A faint mist hangs over the harvest fields around, and the
whole of creation seems to be held in a trance. We breathe in the
moist air of a late summer dawn, ourselves half in a dream as we
move along like wraiths through the mist exhaling from the river.
We position ourselves in different places at the base of the steep
banks and begin to mount our rods, calling out to one another in
subdued voices, excitedly, and for reassurance. Strangely, I have no
memory of what followed in the next three hours, merely impres-
sions deriving from the atmosphere of that early experience, chiefly
the sounds of the river, the musky tang, the occasional stomping
and thundering of young bullocks somewhere out there in the
meadow. As time passed, and the sun appeared and began to warm
away the mist, the earth gradually woke from its trance; trees,
woods, meadows emerged from their mystery and became real. We
began to call to one another in louder voices, as people emerging
from ancient churches forget to whisper and resume their normal
tones. By the time we muster along the bank to return for breakfast a
few hours later we are a confident, chattering crew, all trace of our
earlier "holy dread" vanished like smoke into the sunny air. We
have all had some success. Bream, roach and chub have been taken.
My brother has had the biggest fish, a large chub, and we are all now
confident and eager for more. Breakfast is a feast of ham and eggs in
the little parlour, and we recount our deeds to my two sisters who
promise to join us at the river later in the morning armed with
sketchpads. I still have a pen sketch of How Caple Court done by
one of them. A little faded, it evokes that pre-war time when we
were together in that nimbus of youth, unaware of how soon the
fates would call us apart.

We return after breakfast and by midday have glutted ourselves with success. My own prize is a three-pound trout taken on a worm and destined for the pot because the worm has been gorged and the trout has to be killed. The next morning we are again up early. This time we are all after pike, of which we are told there are some monsters hereabouts. We boast no spinning rods, but we have steel traces, have kept some live bait from the previous day and our floats are large corks from some jars at the farm. All morning we try different "holes" without success. Then, as we gather to return for lunch and collect my brother (always the last to throw in the sponge), his cork disappears with a rush and he is into something which runs like an express, then stops and anchors itself. It cannot be moved. For some time we all think the fish is gone and he is snagged, but another sudden rush confirms that he is still on. My brother winds in whenever he can, then releases line grudgingly as the fish rushes away. Gradually these rushes become less ferocious and shorter in length. Suddenly he is spent and is towed to the bank where we ease him out at our feet. We have no scales but we calculate that he must weigh over fifteen pounds, deep-bellied and with the tail of a quite sizeable jack still protruding from his jaws. My brother takes the long pliers we have optimistically brought with us and shakes the treble from his bony mouth. He is contemplated for a moment by the assembled group with great satisfaction. A gentle shove with my brother's wellington and he is back in his element. We all move off up the bank excitedly chattering.

So the days pass. On Saturday evening Jim, shaved and well supplied with shag for making his cigarettes, leads us off to some place of interest. Bruce, the springer spaniel, disappears into the fastnesses of a field of beet and leaps from plant to plant like a jack-in-the-box, starting rabbits and in his element. By the oil lamp in some cottage pub, where we are the only clients all evening, and the owner had to be found and called in from his garden to serve us, we sit listening to Jim's tales, chiefly answers to our many questions. He had been a prisoner of war in Germany. Almost all his school friends had been killed in that great slaughter. One evening he walked along to the church with us and read out their names. He had a tale to tell of each of them. When he came to the long list of his brothers-in-law he was silent and turned away.

Jim could distinguish between different qualities of spring and well water, and whenever we passed a pump or a stone water-trough he would sample the water and comment appreciatively. Years after, I visited Foy and searched for him. He had left the farm and retired to a cottage at Brampton, not far away along the familiar road. Though slightly plumper he was unchanged. He made me sample the best water for miles around from the well at his cottage door. It tasted like dew. He remembered every detail of the fortnight we spent at the farm, and with a twinkle reminded me of something I thought had been forgotten ... a "fern ticket" he had given me one evening when he passed me while I was deep in converse with the local beauty. He had explained the meaning of the term later, and I recalled it, though I did not blush as then.

The spell of the Wye has remained with me. The tang of those early mornings and misty evenings, the cider and paraffin lamps, have passed beyond the sensory into the affective regions of my being. Standing under those towering riverbanks, my friends and brother similarly employed nearby, my float hanging still, out of the main pull of the current, there was a feeling of at-oneness with those timeless presences of meadows, trees and moving waters. Was it that my father was born and lived his boyhood only three miles away, had been orphaned and transported away to the north before he was in his teens? I felt, and feel some archetypal affinity with the Wye and its soft-spoken people. "How often has my spirit been with thee, O sylvan Wye, thou wanderer through the woods..." One evening I stood at the edge of the river on a long, sweeping bend beyond How Caple. It was on the verge of dusk. I had climbed down the steep cliff to the water's edge and a harvest moon was just showing. There, in the vast, still lagoon of slack water formed by the outside of the bend the large trout were guzzling down the masses of spent flies. They were there to be had by the thousand and the trout were shovelling them down. Suddenly, a hundred yards downstream, a salmon leapt, and its splash echoed. Almost with a sense of primitive fear I climbed back up the cliff and returned to the farm, full of a sense of "unknown modes of being". How friendly was the sound of voices in the farm kitchen as I approached, and the light of the lamp shining out across the river in that thinly populated valley.

15

Charms of Stillwater Fishing

Early in the season, before the river tempts me out (our river wakes up late, and the trout are not out and about until the last days of April) it is to the lakes that I look for my first rod-bending encounters. The day is blustery, but the wind has no edge to it. I arrive at the lake, which lies close to a farm, and greet the farmer. He tells me that there have been one or two cormorants about in the last few weeks; not good news. One of our members has permission to shoot a certain number I am told, and his activities may have scared them away. I can see no sign of them as I sign in and inspect the book. Mine is the only signature so far today. Yesterday several fish have been taken, most of them on lures, and no doubt on sinking lines. I set up with a floating line and a silver-shanked Butcher weighted with a tiny gold-head. I hate fishing with a sinking line All control seems to vanish as the dreary dredging proceeds. Ready! The first cast of the season. How many thousands of them there will be before the lake season closes at the end of November! I feel that exhilaration known to all aficionados of this delightful pastime as I extend the line with a few false casts to explore the nearer water. The wind here blows a gale when elsewhere it is a mere zephyr. I mend the line and look about as I allow the fly to sink. The coots are diving and cavorting in the first joys of spring. How often an apparent rise deceives the unwary novice. Wait a few moments and the coot will emerge nearby, making that sound like a metal punch being hammered. I begin to retrieve, and a sudden burst of sun lights up the whole lake like a searchlight. I tighten the line to cast again and discover that I am into a fish not three yards out. I can see its rainbow flash in the clear lake water. Off it goes, plunging and tugging, the rod bending for the first time this season. When he comes to the net and is weighed he balances at just under two pounds. I release him and away he oars. He is my libation to the gods. The next (if there is one) will be taken for the pot, and the next, and the next. After that, mostly for the rest of the season, I shall fish barbless and have the pleasure of seeing my victims escape to freedom.

Out there, just within range, the water is disturbed in the natural movement of the waves and I guess that a fish is surfacing. Out goes the line. I allow for the wind and the fly kisses the surface not more than a few feet from the target. I begin to move the fly and away it is towed. It dives, and appears twenty yards away, the line in a submerged bend at right angles to where the fish now is. I play it and guess that it must be another two-pounder. Wrong. As I net it, I know I have mistaken vigour for size. It weighs a pound and it goes into my bag for its sins. As I conclude these rites a figure appears and joins me. We shake hands and make the usual enquiries about how the winter has treated us. I have not seen him since the last day of last season but we have often met at this lakeside and I regard him as a friend, though I know nothing of his personal life nor he of mine. We share news, light cigarettes, and he moves across towards the further end of the lake where he is soon hard at work. The wind seems to be dropping and one or two fish begin to show. I replace my Butcher by a Mallard and Claret without the gold-head and aim at where the fish appeared. A dozen or so casts produce no response. There seem to be no flies visible on the surface so I change the fly and attach a small Viva. The rest is easy. Within half an hour I have my full bag and am ready to leave. The cowman appears beyond the fence, calling to his dog. I watch as he rounds up the cows from the farthest corners of the pasture and, guided by the cowman's loud cries, they are ushered in the direction of the cow byre. The cowman comes to the fence to enquire how the fishing is going. I compliment him on the dog's superb performance and his reply is, "E's a magician. I wish I could train 'im to milk the buggers!"

Years ago in summer, in the lakeside reeds clouds of sedges would hatch and fly about. The breeze would disperse them, but some would blow onto the water. It was fine sport to float a dry sedge into the waves not far out and see them seized hungrily. At other times, with a Coachman cast far out to rises, the sport was breathtaking. Often four successive casts would each take a fish. The sad concomitant to this was that, a full bag having been taken, the angler must cease his activities. When this happened he usually went over to where another angler was fishing and sought vicarious pleasure in watching another's efforts. The charm of the sport kept him there and delayed his return home for another hour or two.

In high summer, the lake as still as a sheet of glass, there is little to detain the avid angler. But he is detained. He sees no rises so he fishes deep, with damselfly nymph or Pheasant Tail. Many an hour passes without a take. On one such occasion, having tried a whole range of flies and nymphs, I attached a small corixa. No fish had been seen to rise for hours. Out it sailed, a long cast. It had hardly been jerked twice when it was taken violently, played and brought to the net. The fish returned, my hands dunked and dried, I cast again to about the same spot, and again, this time almost instantly, it was taken. Four successive casts to the same place produced four fish – the prescribed bag limit. How clever, how competent I felt. I now knew the secret of hot, still days in high summer. Attach a corixa, jerk it a few times, and hey presto! Alas, I was young and innocent. Another day, in the same conditions, in the same place, with the same corixa ... nothing.

Later in the season there is the added treat of the crane fly, the daddy-long-legs. Cast him far out over the waves and let him ride free. Watch him as he bobs up and down, carried slowly by the wind, and see him taken. This is as good as fishing the dry sedge. An added charm is to see the long shape as it approaches the riding fly and decides to take it. As Shakespeare puts it (angler that he certainly was):

> "The pleasantest angling is to see the fish
> Cut with her golden oar the silver stream."

Strangely, when the well-cocked crane fly seems not to tempt, provided there are some on the water, it can pay to fish it wet, just submerged. I have found that this is also true of the mayfly. Times without number I have fished upstream in the river to fish rising to the mayfly and not been taken. I have changed the fly in vain. Then, the first time accidentally, the fly submerged and was taken. On such occasions perhaps it is taken as spent, in preference to the surface-fluttering version. When, late in summer, the crane fly does not tempt the fish, a hopper lying on the surface can be seized hungrily, especially if cast near floating weedbanks.

In the dog days, when the river has lost its flow, a visit to the lake for the evening rise can be spectacular. An hour after the sun has left the water is the magic time. I have known some evenings when the fish are rising in hundreds, not a breath of wind stirring, the scene primeval. At such times a tiny pheasant tail nymph, fished on a cast greased to within a foot of the fly, can take trout one after another. Sometimes it pays to move the fly in short pulls. At others it pays to wait a second or two for it to be taken. In my experience the smaller the fly the better. Later, as dusk begins to darken, I sometimes change the fly for a phantom nymph, a mere silver shank. Moved slowly, it is taken when they no longer seem interested in the pheasant tail nymph. Such evenings are the crown of the summer part of the season in lake fishing. There is only one disadvantage. On these occasions one is not alone. The full complement of six is there, arriving at intervals. The company is pleasant, conversation is lively, there is much witty exchange. But the spell of the dusk is broken, and I think of that evening on the Wye beyond How Caple, not a soul about, the trout guzzling, the dusk gathering, and one or two oil lamps lighting in the farms across the valley.

Autumn, to me, is the most exciting and productive season for lake fishing. By the end of September the river season is over. If we are to fish to the end of November it will be on our lakes. It is an appetising prospect. The weed which makes it difficult to fish the lakes in mid-season is long gone. The water is crystal clear, and the trout seem to rise freely on most days. The dry fly is called for and does great execution. Sometimes arrival at the lake is greeted by a veritable plethora of rises. At the edges I can see water boatmen oaring about in tiny jerks and I place on a corixa which imitates this creature. Today is still, and the sun is warm. I cast out gently and tug the fly through the water in tiny movements. A trout surges at it and misses, or changes its mind. I throw the fly out further to another place where a trout has moved and it is taken. A fish of a pound and a half comes to the net and is released. Three more casts move three more fish, two of which I lose (I am fishing barbless). The one which stays hooked has taken the fly at the very end of the retrieve and is a hefty specimen. It takes the line far out, then does a wide arc and returns easily to within yards of where I am standing. I play him gently. A three-pound breaking strain leader must not be

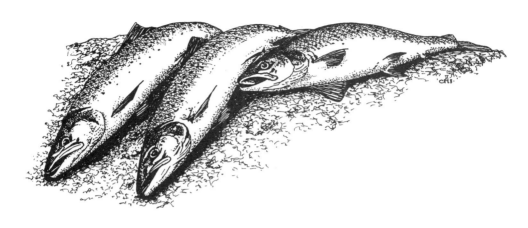

pressured unduly. The reel screeches pleasingly as it oars away into the middle. With no barb on the fly the line must not go slack for a moment. More vigorous tugging, the rod well bent, until gradually he tires and comes to the net. He weighs just over three pounds and is a flashing beauty in perfect condition with a broad tail. I hold him in the water, his gills moving, until suddenly he shoots away and disappears in his element.

I move to a place across the lake and near the end, where I calculate that any flies blown by the wind may have accumulated. Two down and two to go. This is the question that is presented to anglers here at this stage. The bag limit is four fish whether they are returned or not. The man who comes here for a day's fishing is reluctant to take his four fish (on days when this is likely) before half the day is over. This is the moment when he decides to try new tactics and experiment in a way he is not prepared to risk when the going is not so good. What about those Coch y Bondhus lying in his wallet since the days he fished the Onny? This is the time when small beetles are about, and one or two can be seen in the edges. And what about those shrimps he has hardly ever used, with shell-like plastic backs? And those Tups Indispensable which once took large rainbows on a day-ticket lake when no one else did any good? I examine the wallets in a leisurely way. It is one of those pleasant decisions, very different from those I had to make in khaki days when Germans, not trout, were the quarry, and when taken there was no question of returning them. I decide on the little Welsh beetle and cast out towards the middle. I can just see it. Nothing happens. I leave it there for a good minute then retrieve slowly. The moment the little fly moves it is taken with a small explosion in the water and after due time another trout comes to the net – about a pound and a half. I do not weigh it but release it with a sigh and light up. Today, for once, I have brought a flask of sweet coffee and I sit drinking it as I smoke. I rarely, to my regret, bring sandwiches. I watch others, more provident than I, unpacking their pile of sandwiches and offering me a share, which I always refuse: a legacy from army days when it was not the thing to take another's rations. When I leave home for a trip to the water I am usually replete with breakfast, and cannot imagine that I shall be hungry during the rest of the day. Alas! I secretly envy those who have known better and come duly armed.

The shrimp is now attached and cast out. For ten minutes I manoeuvre it as appropriately as I can with no result. I cast out in various places. Once it is snatched at but missed as it touches the water. Another ten minutes and I decide to sack the shrimp and return to the corixa which did so much damage earlier on the other side. I cast our confidently and jerk it through the water. Nothing. I try another part of the lake on the same side, but again to no avail. I am now hungry for the former plenitude, the repeated takes, but nothing happens. So much for overweening self-confidence. I should have continued when the going was good. "We must take the current when it serves Or lose our ventures." How true this is in fishing as in other activities. I move back to the place where the trout were committing suicide when I first arrived and try there again with the corixa. Nothing. That first glorious flush is gone. The lake seems dead. In desperation I attach a Viva lure, let it sink, and tow it slowly back. Two casts later and I am taken, from somewhere deep down. I bring him to the net and return him. He is well over the two-pound mark. But he has been taken on a lure. I break the rod, clip on the net and return to the car. The best of the day is over. I have had good sport and enter my takes and the time in the book.

Anyhow, the sun is gone and the wind is turning sharper. I am on my way home.

One day on the lake remains in my memory as something of a mystery. It was a warm, balmy day in early October. I arrived to find that I had the lake to myself. The water was calm, and a gentle breeze was blowing across the water. I could see no rises, so I decided to dally. I went to the end of the lake, mounted the rod, and opened my fly wallets. For some reason I cannot explain I found among the long-shanks a ragged specimen which a fishing friend had one day called a squirrel tail, a fly, he claimed, which had done him proud on many an occasion such as this. I tied it on, cast out, saw the fifteen-foot leader loop over, and the fly enter the water far out. I settled myself in the grasses, lit a cigarette, and prepared myself to wait for something to rise. The present operation, I was sure, was merely something to do in the interval. I made no retrieve, but watched as the breeze moved the end of the line slowly across the water. Suddenly the rod bent, the reel screeched, and the line was picked up in a spray as it was taken far out to the middle of the lake. It took five minutes to play, the rod bent steeply, the reel alternately whizzing round, pausing, then being wound back. At last I brought to the net a rainbow seven pounds in weight and in perfect, gleaming condition. I detached the fly and held this beauty in the water until it was recovered, and saw it at last streak away with a sweep of its broad tail.

The fly, a little the worse for wear, was duly dried and dusted and again cast out well to the left so that the wind could again move it across the lake at its own speed. This pleasant surprise had alerted my senses. I decided that letting the fly move only at the speed dictated by the breeze had perhaps accounted for this unexpected success. I held the rod, this time more expectant, but convinced that what had happened was one of those "one-offs" which occur unaccountably. At this point in my account I must revert to the present tense, so compulsive is this occasion in memory As the line moves across I see it slide, then suddenly disappear, the rod bends, and again I am into a heavy fish. It runs far out, then across, and again takes several minutes to tire enough to begin easing its way reluctantly to the net. Another rainbow, this time just under six pounds. I am filled with that sense of heady self-confidence which all anglers have felt on such occasions. How clever I am! How wise of me to choose just the right fly for this perfect October day! How wise of me to let the wind do the work for me! The fly is now even worse for wear. It is duly dried and dusted. I pause and notice that nowhere is there any sign of a fish rising. I cast out again, a long cast, seat myself once more, and wait for the wind to tow the line slowly across. Dare I say it? As the line reaches the centre in a gentle bend it disappears again and the same ritual follows. Five minutes later another large rainbow comes to the net; over seven pounds, even heavier than the first. I am now in dreamland. Has the sun given me a touch of hyper vision? I note that so far I have not done any retrieving and have had three big fish in three casts. The fly is now ragged in the extreme. I bless it as I dry and dust it. I could eat it myself!

I cast far out to the same place and sit, this time quite tense with expectation as the fly sinks and the wind begins its gentle movement of the line. Gentle reader, I am not given to lying or to exaggeration. As it reaches the same point in its travels it is suddenly skimmed over the water in a shower of spray and a large trout leaps out and plunges back at right angles to where the line was a moment ago. This time I have a longer tussle. When it finally comes to the net it weighs a mere five and a quarter pounds, a veritable tiddler! That is my bag limit. I have to desist. I shall always wonder what would have happened if I had continued this almost hypnotic sequence of cast-and-wait. I pack my things, break the rod and amble back to the car in a haze of October sun and hubris. If there were a red carpet along the lake I would not hesitate to tread it all the way!

16

Fishing the Dorsetshire Piddle and Frome

I am in a thatched cottage on the edge of Egdon Heath in the heart of Hardy country. It is early August and I am agog with vague anticipations and uncoordinated plans for a week of fishing these delicious chalk streams. I have boiled a couple of eggs and demolished them with slices of bread and butter, drunk several cups of tea, stowed my kit in appropriate places, washed and changed into suitable attire, and am about to sally forth and seek out the proprietor with whom I have arranged the fishing. Half a mile away I find him, busy with a small group, presumably of beginners in the gentle art, instructing them in how to cast. He breaks them off to practise for a few minutes and joins me with a friendly greeting. I arrange with him where I can fish on various days and on which beats. He gives me maps, answers all my questions, and wishes me well as he joins his group of acolytes. I have the impression of a very charming fellow, and we have parted on Christian name terms. He will be here to consult whenever I need his advice. I pause for a few minutes to look round his cabin close to the house where he lives, and admire the setting of lawns, trees and outbuildings. In the cabin is every type of fly-fishing gear, together with cases of flies. Of these I make a small selection and pay the lady, presumably his wife, who answers my call. Time to wander off and do a local recce for tomorrow's activities.

At this season I would not normally hope for much sport with the dry fly, but here, on these ever-runny, surging streams, I am confident that things will be different. The Piddle is only a few hundred yards away across a meadow. In between are several large trout lakes where I am told I can fish at any time without further booking. So, when (or if) I tire of the river, or fancy a change of activity, there are plenty of possibilities here. I notice as I skirt one of the lakes that there are plenty of large fish oaring about and occasionally rising with casual confidence. As I reach the river I pause and my eyes wander to the sunlit distances of Egdon Heath. It is all I had imagined, instinct with the mood of the novels and the characters who haunted it, and with whom I have been acquainted from early days.

At last, the river. I cross a tiny footbridge and startle a lusty trout that disappears with a wave of the clear water. Despite the season it is welling full and urgent through the cresses and weed. As I stand and take it all in there is a confident rise just upstream, then another, this time a swerving take which seems to indicate that a sedge has just been swallowed. It is now early evening, and I am beginning to regret that I am here without the necessary tools. I reassure myself that it is far better to know the stretch, explore its whole length, than to begin operations blind to what lies ahead. I move on. At every stage of my recce new vistas unfold. Here there is a bend where the gravel shines warm and clean through four feet of water; further on is a sort of sink below a point where there is a surge of water entering from a point two feet above. Further on there are short reaches of dimpling, shallow water flanked with flowering weeds, mimulus and bright kingcups. I explore the reach to its limit, and walk quickly across the meadow, flanking the lakes until I reach the bottom of the stretch. Again I move upstream and continue my exploration of this new wonderland. Here the river is deeper and broader, easier to cast from positions of concealment. Quite a number of trout are moving by now. As the evening grows into dusk there are several sedge rises. The bow waves from these travel to me along the surface as I watch and continue my now crouching progress. At last I am back at the little footbridge where I began an hour or two ago. Dusk is now hanging over the whole of Egdon Heath, and fingers of mist have drifted over the river behind me. I trudge back across the meadow to the road and walk on to the cottage where I am staying for the week. I try to plan for tomorrow. Certainly I must fish the river in the evening. But can I resist trying it in the morning? And when shall I go into Dorchester for supplies? At last I decide. I shall fish the river for a few hours in the morning, then have an hour or two before midday on the lakes. Off to Dorchester for lunch and supplies, and, of course, a quick mooch around that fabled town. Afterwards, back to the cottage for an hour or two, and a look around, with perhaps a visit to the bridge not far away which I have seen on the map, where I can see what the river is like below my beat. Then, with rod and waders, I shall wander the length of the beat I have explored today.

I am up bright and early, but not as early as I had planned. The general excitement of yesterday must have tired me more than I had expected, and I have slept soundly. Bacon and eggs with buttered toast have fortified me, and I collect my tackle. Outside the air is fragrant, and my watch tells me it is eight o'clock. The grass across the meadow is wet with the dew of the night, and Egdon Heath is wakening as the August sun warms the valley. I skirt the lakes and arrive at the river. All lies before me. Here is a chalk stream waiting for my advances, and I pause to ponder on what fly to tie on. Nothing is rising, but the river is surging and welling as urgently as ever. "I slip, I slide, I gloom, I glance.." the words come to mind from the hinterland of memory as I search my wallet and tie on a B.W.O., the Blue-winged Olive which used to do such execution on the Kentish Stour by whose banks I once lived, another chalk stream of loved memory. Ahead is a gliding stretch, and I cast the fly lightly upstream and let it float back to me in the hope that a trout may catch sight of an early morsel and be tempted. No response. I cast again, three or four times to no effect. Shall I try a nymph, or a shrimp? I decide not. I edge a yard or two away from the bank and move slowly upstream in the hope of seeing something rising. There is no sign of anything. Small wonder. There are no flies hatching, and at every tempting reach opening before me the surface remains untroubled by surfacing fish. I walk slowly on, and eventually arrive at the little footbridge. I cross it and continue a good way beyond. The bends and riffles, the glides and freshets show no sign of the finny prey.

As I continue upstream I am beginning to wonder if it is time to resort to the submerged nymph when just ahead where the stream bends and forms the sink (noted yesterday) I see a fish move. At the head of the sink the river is a foot higher, and the stream pours down in a graceful curve into it. I crouch and cast up the long, narrow approach to the sink and land the fly gently just below where the water enters. I am not prepared for the sudden response. The fly is snatched and is tightened as the trout, a good one, having no means of escape upstream, arrows back to where I am standing and escapes before I can tighten on the slack. I look downstream and see the wave as my escaped trout seeks other quarters. No matter, the encounter has encouraged me. I have made contact, however briefly, and I rose the fish. I move on upstream. A hazy sun is filling the day with gentle warmth and the air is still. Up there, under a bank where the river creams round in a smooth surge, and the amber bed can be seen as I crouch low, I can just make out a shape in mid-water. Is it one of those trailing weeds so easily mistaken by the eager angler for what he is on the lookout for? I galvanize and wait for a sign of movement. There is a regular undulation, but is it a fish? For five whole minutes (or so it seems) I hover, keyed up with expectation. As I strain my eyes a shape darts a foot across the current and immediately resumes station. I was right. It is a trout, and it is feeding. Some nymph especially tempting must have attracted it to swerve a foot off course. Can I tempt it to rise to something on the surface? I have my doubts. Even my light leader may startle him as it passes over him, especially with the sun providing a shadow as thick as a rope. I degrease my leader, apply line-sink, remove the B.W.O. and replace it with a weighted Pheasant tail nymph. If I cast it to land just a couple of feet ahead, and the same to the right, as lightly as possible, it may just be visible to my friend up there. But there is the danger that my rod movement may be seen. No false casting then, and the rod must be held well above the butt. There is no obstacle to the right, and the banks are low, so I may be able to cast obliquely, the rod at a two o'clock angle. So here goes. The nymph sails out, touches the water a yard ahead of the target, and quietly sinks. It moves in the current well to the right of where the trout is likely to see it. I gather in line and cast again. This time it glides past the hovering form not six inches from his nose. The fish makes a slight gesture towards it and declines the offer. I gather back the leader and pause to consider. I shall cast a little further upstream to give time for the nymph to sink, then raise the rod so that the nymph will heave up as it passes the trout's nose. If that fails I shall try another fly, perhaps a shrimp.

Out goes the line and the nymph enters the water a good six feet ahead of the feeding trout. I raise the rod, the nymph rises, and suddenly the rod is bent double. I stand up and struggle to keep the fish out of the weeds ahead. He comes round then darts towards me, but I am prepared for this and tighten as he reaches where I stand and anchors himself upstream, under the bank where he has been feeding. One or two more efforts on his part and I am able to get his nose out of the water and hold him, then down he comes to the net. I lift him to the grass, detach the nymph, and survey him briefly before returning him to where he belongs. He is a magnificent two-pounder, "rose moles all in stipple", a gleaming beauty. Good luck to him. I straighten up, light a cigarette, and look around. It is as if I had forgotten my surroundings, and the quiet charm of this lovely stream, above and below where I stand, begins to assert itself. I look around, drinking it in, replete as the trout I have just temporarily removed from his morning pursuits. Morning? I glance at my watch and realise with surprise that it is almost midday. The time has come for me to move on. In the evening I shall come here again, hoping that the dry fly will come into its own.

I walk across the meadow, leaving the little river to its own music. Just time for a brief skirmish on one of the lakes. As I approach I can see one or two fish moving. What a comble de richesse! And how delightful is a change of activity in this world of waters and meadows and hazy sun. My lake rod is at the cottage but my eight-foot Bruce and Walker will be enough for the moment. I attach a fifteen-foot leader and a corixa and cast out. I pull it with gentle three-inch tweaks to imitate the water boatman. A fish moves at the side of a bank of weed not far out and I land the fly near it. There is a swirl and the fish is on. I play it, letting the reel screech as it urges away over the lake. The rod is bent almost double and I think I am into something quite big. As the fish tires I am about to bring his nose up out of the water when he dives down and is into submerged weed. Not knowing the lake I cannot know where the clear spots are. I feel I am about to lose him. In these circumstances it always seems best to slacken the tension and hope that the fish will move out of the weed of its own accord. This time I am lucky; the line tightens again as the trout swims away. I bring his nose up firmly and ease him towards me. He does one or two more lunges but he is tired and at last comes to the net. I weigh him in the net and release him. Deducting the weight of the net I find he was three and a half pounds, and in excellent condition with broad tail and splendid girth. I wind in, stow the fly, break the rod and set off back to the cottage.

Thatched cottages are cool in summer and warm in winter, they say. The summer part of this seems to be true. There is a pleasant, exciting smell about the place. In the garden the apple trees are loaded, and there is a litter of fallen fruit at their feet where wasps and bees are busy making the most of the feast. I change my clothes, and after a quick sluice and a glass of the beer I have (for once) had the foresight to bring down here with me, I am ready to set off for Dorchester. There I shall buy provisions (I am no cook, so these will be very basic) and have lunch. On the way from the cottage I shall go the few hundred yards to the bridge half a mile below my fishing to see what the river is like there. Off I go. It has been a splendid renewal of my chalkstream experience and I am still taken with surprise at finding waters so clear and urgent in their wellings and brimmings, even so late in the season. The growths of flowering weed are themselves dazzling and fresh as the waters that swell around them, and the bed over which they wave with the currents can be seen glowing with that saffron tint I have seen on the fluted columns of ancient Greek temples in southern Italy. Above all, it is the translucency of the water which still surprises after the "dim suffusion" of more northern streams. Writers complain about the changes in the water table of the chalkstreams, and the diminishing of that crystal clarity they once had. I well remember looking down from the bridge over the Test at Barton Stacey where I was stationed for a while during the war and being amazed at the clarity of the water. It was as if the huge trout there were hanging suspended in air. This morning I have looked into waters no less pellucid ... or so it seems to me.

I arrive at the bridge and look eagerly down. It is a low bridge and I feel close to what is going on there as I search the water upstream. Here the river has grown in stature during the half mile of its wanderings and there is, in the reach I am searching, a good four feet of depth. Five yards away I see a lusty two-pounder a foot down, riding the current, moving upwards, slipping an inch or two sideways as it takes the nymphs which seem to be providing a regular diet for this experienced operator. I gaze, fascinated. A yard or two ahead, zig-zagging with gay insouciance, a large sedge is cavorting to and fro across the water. As the current brings it down towards me, my nymphing friend suddenly darts across with a great swirl and the sedge is gone, leaving a mighty ring in the water. As the disturbance subsides, and the surface regains its placid habit, I can see my trout is back in his feeding station and taking the regular supply of nymphs once more. The sedge was a titbit it could not resist. But it expended far more energy on its lunge to the sedge than it needs in its present nymphing position, with its guaranteed supply of food with no effort required.

Time to move on. I leave the bridge and drive through a small cluster of thatched cottages on towards a larger house sitting close to the river. I stop the car and look over the garden with its broad swim of river flowing through it. Happy owner, I think – beatus ille! And yet, long ago when I was too fraught with my affairs to appreciate it, I too once lived in a house whose lawns sloped gently down to a chalkstream in Kent. It now seems like a dream. I sigh and drive on. Enough of this; I am hungry, and Dorchester is waiting for me a few pleasant miles away.

The town is busy, but Hardy is here in every nook and cranny for me. I have crossed the Frome, lunched in an old inn, discovered in a bookshop one of my books, recently published, and signed it. This seems to be one of those days on which everything goes right! I take my list and buy my provisions. I have visited the Hardy museum. I must not dally. This is no time to be musing with the far-away and long-ago. The sun is now hot. Mid-August in all its plenitude sits on the little town and steeps all the countryside of Dorset. I find the car, open the windows, and am on my way back to my other pursuits.

As I arrive, there is some activity at one of the lakes which borders the lane to the cottage. Unlike the others it has an overplus of weed which is now in the process of being removed. A youth who helps the proprietor with the various chores involved in keeping things in trim is swimming out, towing behind him a length of dragnet. He manages a long haul, a rope is thrown, and the net with hundredweights of weed is towed in to the side. I leave, reminding myself to call each day to enter my doings in the book. I am lucky that at this season there will be no problem with booking beats on the various stretches of the river, and of the Frome. Arrived at the cottage I bestow my provisions in appropriate places, make a pot of tea and wander into the garden. I select a shady spot, drink my tea, and stretch out. All around are the sounds of a late summer day, heady and soporific. I drink them in and am soon lost to it all in the arms of Morpheus. The sun must have moved the shade where I am lying. I shake off my slumber and look at my watch. I have been asleep for at least two hours and feel that welcome, relaxed satisfaction known only to those who rarely sleep during the day. I stagger to my feet and go in to make something to nourish the inner man before setting out to try the river when the sun is off the water.

Seven o'clock. With rod and waders I walk along to the river, happy that I have already made its acquaintance and know some of its likely places. A great quiet has drifted down over Egdon Heath and the whole amphitheatre in which I am a tiny figure seems to be holding its breath. Whatever happens I feel that it is enough to be here among the moistening tangs of the evening, a part of its timeless spell.

Before tackling up at the downstream end of the beat I pause to examine the water ahead. Almost immediately a ring appears twenty yards upstream. What to attach? I decide on a grey duster, parachute-tied. The lighter the fly touches the surface on these waters the better. I false cast to get the line out, well away from the river so that the line will not be seen by the feeding trout, then change direction and am lucky to "land" the fly a yard ahead of where I saw the rings. Was it a "oncer"? The fly floats back to me untouched. I cast three times with no sign of a take. Surprisingly, and to my relief, the fish rises again. I have not put it down. I haul in the line and change the fly for a B.W.O., universally taken on the Kentish Stour until late evening when the sedges were out. I dip it in flotant, whisk it about, and cast out to where the rings appeared It trembles for a moment, and as it begins its journey in the current it is taken with quiet, unrushed assurance by my unsuspecting quarry. What a fight it puts up It is whole minutes of reel screechings and rod bendings as it oars upstream, changes its mind, rushes back towards me and noses into weeds before I have it more or less under control and bring it to the net. It is a pound and a half of lively resilience and I return it to the water to resume its ways uninterrupted.

As I straighten and look upstream I hear likely sounds coming from just round the next bend. The sun is now off the meadows and as I approach the place where the sound came from I see a short, clear reach where sedge are in the air. I lose no time in replacing the fly and tying on a sedge, this time a small Coachman. No need to grease the fly. Dusk is gathering, and with the sedge there is no need for the finesse required with other flies. I throw it out, rod held high so that the minimum of line is in the water, and draw it over the surface in short darts. It is taken in moments. The trout darts into the reeds at the edge and despite all my efforts to get him free, I am broken. Further upstream there is another commotion, and another just beyond. I quickly tie on another Coachman and move up. This time I shall do my best to avoid the edges if I am taken. Here the river is a little wider, so we shall see. I cast up towards the rise, rod high, and drift the fly across. Again it is taken, and this time the fish oars upstream in a series of heavy lunges. As soon as I can I ease his nose up, but again he dives away. Now he is bent on getting as far away as possible, and the line goes out as he moves further and further upstream. With a light leader there is nothing to be done but give him his head while applying enough strain to restrain him, but not enough to break the three-pound nylon. I get his nose up and flounder him along the surface with enough slack to pay out instantly if he makes another lunge. He is tired now, and after a few feebler efforts he comes to the net. Just under two pounds.

As I release him and straighten, I am aware that the dusk is deepening around. In the half-light I can now hear many of those sounds of fish rising to sedge which are such a delight to the angler at dusk. When I was rowing in eights on the Cam, our coach urged us to jump the blade of the oars in, making the oars bend and producing the desired "bell note". These sedge rises remind me of the bell notes of those distant days. I hurry on upstream, knowing that in half an hour or less (or more, I hope) it will all be over, and the river will suddenly go dead. I have my pen torch with me, necessary for tying on the fly in the gathering dark.

The surface of the river is now only a glimmer and distances are hard to calculate. The effect is almost hypnotic, making the eyes narrow in order to focus. I throw the fly upstream, less caution now needed, and with rod held high, dap the fly to and fro. Two or three casts more as I move on upstream and again I am into a fish. Eyesight is now less important than sense of touch, and as always on such occasions I am surprised how much easier it is to co-ordinate movements when the eyes are less involved. I manoeuvre the fish by sense of touch only. I can hardly see where he is, but I can sense when he is moving and when he is anchored, and bring him almost to the net like a blind man. Alas! At the last moment in the tussle he makes a final effort and throws himself in the air, lands in the reeds and is off. A good fish too. Had I been able to see more clearly in these last rites, he would have been guided into the waiting net. I must have missed by inches. I stumble on about twenty yards, and guided by the sounds of another violent rise, I pause, position myself, and make a decision.

At the edge of dark, especially when trout are going for the sedge, a heavier leader is called for. Reeds and lack of visibility are in the trouts' favour. Aiming and playing are more or less "chuck and chance it" routines. That fatal sense of a broken cast can play havoc with the mind of the angler who is both set on bringing in a fish, and at the same time tempted to allow it too free a rein in case he should be broken. In haste I grip the torch in my mouth and set about uncoiling a five-pound leader and attaching it to the line This is accomplished with much unseemly cursing by someone who seems to be me, and the Coachman is attached after much poking at the eye of the fly. I pick myself up and, more confident now, throw it out upstream into the gathering shadows. Not a movement, not a sound. I tow it, splash it, skitter it as temptingly as I know how. There is no response. I straighten up and look around. All is silent. A slight wisp of mist is descending on the river. No trout are rising. The river is dead. It is over. There is that familiar sense that further effort will be unavailing. I wind in, hook up the fly and move off across the darkling meadow. As I skirt one of the lakes I note that it, too, has gone to sleep. When I arrive back at the cottage and look out at the garden I note that it, too, is dead, or rather, at this hour of mystery, dreaming, perhaps waiting for the harvest moon to bring it back into the light.

Day two. I am off for a few hours on a beat of the same river a few miles away. I have instructions and a useful sketch map. In my bag are a few things to sustain me, and in my heart a great sense of that pleasure at the thought of exploring new waters. I arrive at the fishing hut having crossed a bit of heath and move to the river. Nothing is showing, but the river here is quite wide and in full flow. I intend to walk downstream to the end of the beat and then fish up in the hope that in an hour or two one or two fish may be surfacing. A mile or two of beautiful waters, now broad and dimpling, now narrowing into bends and riffles. Around me are meadows and dingles, and everywhere the sounds of running water. I have come during a spell of warm, windless days, of hazy sun that grows stronger as the day advances. I finally reach the end of the beat where the river narrows and disappears into a thicket. I have passed under a bridge, and after a short rest I shall move up there to explore in likely places. The scene is like a wild garden. There is willow herb among the grasses, yellow mimulus, purple loosestrife where bees are having a late forage, and a dozen others which for me are nameless.

As I take it all in I can hear the sound of splashy rises somewhere ahead. I move up along the bank and settle down to watch. I can see one or two damselflies hovering here and there, gleaming with that kingfisher blue of their iridescent wings. Suddenly, a few yards up the bank where I stand, a trout shoots up half out of the water and seizes the damselfly hovering an inch above the surface. I have seen this only once before, on one of our lakes, on a hot summer day. I was watching the damselflies hovering when the same thing happened. I continue to watch. The current runs swift near the bank, but I guess that somewhere there the trout has a pocket of slack water where it can lie waiting for something passing close by in the swifter water. Sure enough, as one of the damselflies hovers a couple of feet out, my trout darts at it and the fly is gone with only a flash of broad tail to mark the place. Shall I put on a damselfly nymph? The situation is too tempting to resist. I tie one on, kneel well back, and place the nymph just a yard ahead of the exact spot where I know the trout is lying. The water is too boisterous there for me to see beneath the surface. It returns back to me swiftly in the fast water and I cast again. Again there is no response. I take the nymph and grease both it and a yard of leader. I shall cast it on the surface to the spot where the last one was taken. Instead of laying it on the water I dap it, holding the leader mostly out of the water. The trout surges out and the rod bends. It comes to the net, a very plump, stubby pounder. I have surprised myself. It was a long shot, one of those lucky chances, and I congratulate myself. I know there are no hermetic rules in angling, only general ones. See a situation, calculate the odds, note what is happening, and try it out. It will probably work only once. In this case the trout was feeding on the odd damselflies appearing in his window. I knew exactly where he was and, having no dry damsel, I made the nymph appear like the emerged version and it worked, merely because in such fast water the trout had no time for a leisurely inspection.

I move on towards the bridge. There is current below the two stone piers, and slack water between. A few olives are appearing, some on the water. Nothing appears to be moving, but across on the other side where the water runs smooth and clear there is a rise, followed in a few moments by another. I move back down and watch. I can see a long shape undulating about a foot down, but between me and it are the various fast currents interspersed with slack water where there is probably a deal of back eddy. To get a dry fly to pass over him will require some manoeuvring. I manage to wade out a yard or two having attached an Iron Blue and make a few trial casts well away from where monsieur is feeding (fairly regularly, I note). The trick seems to be to cast up and quickly mend the line so that the fly floats at the tip of a horseshoe, well ahead of the line. To avoid drag, I must peel off a yard or two of line. In this way, I find that I have a chance of passing the fly over him without drag and without the presence of line. Another trial cast and I concentrate on the big one. I see the fly quite clearly as it wobbles, well cocked, four feet this side of his lie. I let the line pass well downstream so as not to startle him and cast again. Perfect. I watch as the fly trembles on its way. I can see the trout. It galvanises, and with the easy assurance of long habit, head up and then tail, it swallows the fly. I pause, tighten, and the struggle is on. This will be easier than last night on a narrower stretch with weed at the edges. He is a good fish and he swims out to the centre, back to where he was taken, then like an arrow, off he goes downstream. I follow him down and bring him back towards me, the rod bent and the reel at its most hysterical pitch. The tussle gradually eases and I bring him in, net him, and place him on the grass. What a beauty; just short of two and a half pounds and in perfect condition, splendid spots and broad tail.

Back he goes, and after a few seconds held in my hands for him to recover he shoots off back into his watery home.

I resume my progress. There is plenty of river to explore and I am in no hurry. A few medium olives and iron blues are coming down. As I look at the water I am struck by the brilliance of the gravel between the weed beds and the clarity of the stream as it purls on its way. The bed has a bright, saffron hue which dazzles the eye and gladdens the heart. To be here, in such a place, and on such a day is sufficient in itself. I move along and come to a short reach where the river narrows and runs deeper. It is here, in two years' time, that I shall be fishing with a friend on the longest day of the year. I describe it as it happened, a year or two ahead of the present events.

I am here to fish the rise on the eve of midsummer. By nine o'clock the sun is still lingering but has left the water. The air is still, and there is no sense of that evening chill. Fish are rising all over, and the bell sounds they make set the fingers twitching. Olives are on the water and the fish are taking them. I cast my ginger quill lightly over a spot a little ahead of where the nearest of them is feeding. There is a perfunctory inspection and no take. I try again with the same result. Time to change the fly. A couple of refusals are hint enough that this is not what they are taking. I replace the fly with another ginger quill, the smallest I can find, and cast again. This time it is taken and after a couple of seconds the fish is off. I dry and grease the fly and move on to where a lusty fish is busy mopping up the provender which is sailing down in such abundance. Again I am taken, and again the fish is lost. Every rise I aim at on this reach results in the same way. Am I tightening too quickly? Hardly. I am allowing the trout to go down before I strike, and I am sure the tightening is not too violent. After six or seven misses I examine the fly, sharpen the point, and try again. The fly must be the right one, else why should it be taken? The rise is just under my bank, a big fish, I guess. I cast badly, landing the fly a good yard beyond where he lies, but it is taken viciously and within seconds he is across and into a bed of weed. He is still on, and I ease the strain in the hope that he will emerge of his own accord. For thirty seconds there is no sign of movement, then with a sudden lunge he is out and upstream like a speedboat then into a bank of weed where he breaks me and is off. I attach a light olive tied parachute-wise and move on, frustrated and puzzled. So far I have botched things. The rise is spectacular, yet so far I have not netted a single fish.

Round the bend is another good reach where the water seems weed-free and the current brisk. I watch a trout as it comes up to a fly with easy grace. My first cast hooks him and after a brief interval he comes to the net. My confidence is restored. One and a half pounds. The parachute must be the answer. Perhaps the other fly failed to cock, making the angle such that it failed to hook when taken. Who can tell? In the next half-hour I net seven fish, the largest two and a half pounds. I am in the process of playing my latest fish when I hear a sudden cry from a distance downstream where my friend, a beginner, relatively speaking, has been at work in vain. I release the fish and as his calls grow more desperate, climb out and run down to where the sounds come from. I find him on his back, legs in the air, and river water pouring out of his waders. He is outraged at the time it has taken me to respond. It seems he had fallen in the river on his back. As he cannot swim he thought he was going to drown. He has lost his glasses, his rod and his net and is in a state of shocked protest at all things in creation. I do my best to console him. I find his glasses, his rod and his net. I tell him that the river is nowhere deep enough to drown him, and here it runs at only three or four feet. All in vain. For him the evening's fishing is over. He has not had a single take and he is wet and miserable. The evening is warm and windless, and at this time of year there will be several hours of fishing still to be done. My entreaties are in vain. The evening's fishing is over for him, and, since we have come in the same car, also over for me. I look at the river ahead longingly, then accompany him as he hurries, large and distraught, the mile or so back to the waiting car. As we move by a hedge a deer leaps over and heads away in front of us. As we reach the heath where the fishing hut stands, dozens of glow-worms light up the furze where they lie. Damp and disconsolate in the car he rouses from his apathy as we see a large badger trotting on ahead of us, lit by the headlamp beams. We follow it for half a mile, almost to the cottage, where at the top of a long incline it turns into a wood where we turn right, and disappears. It is at this spot where I now stand that these events are to take place in the magic of a night in midsummer two years hence.

I am as yet unaware of these delights to come as I continue up the verges of this lovely stream. It is a day to remember, late in the season though it is. What a blessing that there is no wind, not even a slight breeze. Here and there I continue to take fish as the day advances. At a place where the river brims wide and then enters a narrow glen where a bridge over the road constricts it into a deep, fast-running brook, I sit on a boulder and begin to devour my ill-made but welcome sandwiches, but still with both eyes glued to the river ahead. Why is it that, however hungry, I can never resist the lure of rising trout until late in the proceedings? Here where I am lying there is a strong fragrance, and I notice that my waders are cushioned in a bed of water mint. Ahead, in a deeper run just below the little bridge, my eyes pick out a long, dark shape about two feet down. He is immobile, and there is only an occasional movement of his broad tail when the current dictates. He is a heavy, lusty chap, and obviously sole proprietor of this special run with its easy supply of provender. But at the moment he is not feeding. It is as if he were in a post-prandial, somnolent lethargy, oblivious to everything and a little world-weary! None the less, I must not let his slumbers go undisturbed.

I tie on a mayfly nymph in the hope that it will get down to where he is lying. I can't afford to line him by casting too far beyond him in order to give space for the nymph to sink to his level. My plan is to cast and raise the rod before the line touches the water. My fear is that he might become aware of the upraised rod and bolt. I retreat downstream as far as I can without losing sight of where he lies, and throw out the nymph. I see it come slowly back, a yard to his right. Either he has not seen it, or he is not interested. I try again. This time the nymph passes within an inch of his nose. His only response is to move an inch or so to the side, then resume his former position. I gather in the cast and detach the M.F.N. Among my nymphs in the wallet I discover a large creeper, something like a spider, all tendrils and hairy extravagances. It is weighted and will sink quickly. Perhaps if it can come into his window, bumping and grazing the gravel ahead, I might raise it a little as it approaches him. Surely he cannot resist so delicate a morsel. I could eat it myself! Out it goes, up goes the rod, and the creeper trundles down towards him. The nose of the trout comes up, inspects, and as I twitch it, it is swallowed and the water becomes a maelstrom. The line goes out, cutting the water. Under the bridge it anchors briefly, then away again. I am certain to lose him. I stumble upstream to the bridge and manage to turn him as he pauses in a straight, shallow glide ahead. Suddenly the line goes slack as he rushes back downstream towards me. I raise the rod high and pull in the slack, and am amazed that he is still on, almost at my feet. What a beauty! Now he is off again downstream and I am stumbling after him, more confident now that in this stretch of comparatively snag-free water I shall be able to get his nose up and gain the upper hand. Alas! He is full of the desire to be free. As I bring him round he shoots off into the edge, twists himself round a small outcrop of weed and breaks me. It is over. Consummatum est! He is gone, all three-and-a-half to four pounds of him, and I am left with that familiar feeling of triumph and loss. I beguiled him, and he beat me. The river purls on, all passion spent. I reel in, hook up the creeper. The warm sun is westering and it is time to go. I make my way back to the car, glutted and replete with that vague sense of fulfilment all anglers know. The fact that I lost the best fish of the day in no way lowers my spirits as I amble slowly back to the car. I deceived him into a take when he was otherwise not in the mood, and that is enough. I notice that along the reaches as I walk by no fish are rising. I have had the best of this balmy August day.

I have seen on the map the proprietor has provided me with, among other beats of this charming river, a place which charms me with its tempting name: Coolese. (My memory may be at fault at this distance in time; perhaps it was Coolease, or Coolees ...) I decide that this afternoon I shall wander along the lanes and tracks to the ford indicated on the map, and in shirtsleeves, for this is again a hot August day, explore the river's meanderings in cool ease...

The approaches are ripe with the abundance of late summer, and the sketch map helps me to find the river at last. I arrive at the shallow ford, park the car, don my waders and look up and down. Upstream the river enters a deeper glide under some trees and bends away out of sight. Downstream it burbles and saunters between low banks for half a mile or so. I wade across and walk down to the limit where it enters a small copse. After my Shropshire river with its steep banks and (at this season) low water and sluggish current, it is exhilarating to walk along barely a foot or so above the briskly-flowing water level, and to note its clarity, the pebbly bottom and still vivid freshness of the weed banks. I keep well clear, and reach the limit where I mount the rod and search the wallet for inspiration. I shall try various places to the top limit, taking care not to wade and disturb the water, so that I can return down and fish it up more searchingly. I tie on a small blue-winged olive, dunk it, and begin casting. The water surface is boisterous here, and the river wide enough to enable me to aim at likely places to left, right and centre. There are no rises, but if I have no responses at various places on my way up I shall return and try an upstream wet fly or a nymph. I have deliberately omitted to ask the friendly proprietor about the best flies for this stretch, and shall have only myself to blame if I have no response from its inmates. To sail unknown seas has a charm of its own, and as a stranger I feel it right to be alone at the wheel on this voyage of discovery.

C. M. bhenwood.

There is a small movement at the edge, ten yards ahead, then another and another. The fly sails over and touches the water just ahead. There is the slightest sign of an inspection, and the fly returns to my feet. Another cast, and this time no inspection. I remove the B.W.O. and tie on a small spent gnat. I do not oil it, but dunk it in the water so that it will float in the film or just below it. Out it goes and is taken instantly. How easy it is to play a fish on this unencumbered reach. I am pulled vigorously upstream, then across, and am soon holding a gleaming little spotted leopard of a fish, nose up, and guiding it to the net. It is a lovely specimen of about three-quarters of a pound, and it returns to its haunts like an arrow. So often, in my experience, a dry fly in the film, not riding on it, succeeds when fish are not taking floating flies. I move on, not wading, but edging up the bank five or six yards, casting to likely places, and kneeling low, so that I disturb the water as little as possible. Important, because I shall return and fish here again. If nothing is rising I shall fish wet, but in the hope that as the afternoon wears on into early evening some fish may start rising. At several places on the way up I move fish. Sometimes they take and are brought to the net, at others they reject the fly. Sometimes a fish takes the fly two or three yards below where it was first inspected, and on one occasion, almost at my feet. They are all about the same size as the first, but in splendid condition. By the time I arrive at the ford I am warm and thirsty, the sun still hot, but westering. I wade across and go to the car where, for once, I have taken the precaution of placing a cool-box (the name "Coolese" perhaps produced this unusual foresight) and there, propped in the shade, I stay myself with flagons and munch crusty rolls and cheese. This is indeed an idyll. "O qui me gelidis convallibus Haemi sistat." *O for one to lay me in the cool dells of Haemus*. No better place to be, on such a day, at such an hour.

But "à nos moutons," as my French master used to say after one of his many interesting digressions. Evening is coming on, and there is work to be done, if such pleasant chores can be called work. As I prepare to recross the ford and repair downstream, to my right, in the shadowed water where it comes through the trees, there is a lusty rise. I watch, fascinated, as another rise sends large rings down towards me. This looks like a good fish. What to tie on? This fish is taking something on the surface. I detach the spent gnat and tie on a Sherry Spinner, oil it well, and move into position. The place to which I am casting is in shadow, and the water is smooth and slow moving. I shall need to be careful, especially on the withdrawal. The slightest splash and he will be away. I do two or three false casts to get the line out, then shoot the fly. The cast extends perfectly, and the fly kisses the water three feet ahead of where the trout rose but too far to the right. It comes back slowly, trembling and perfectly cocked. I raise the rod so that as the line reaches the current just below it will not drag the fly. I am about to pull back and cast again when there is a swirl just as the fly is about to speed up as it enters the shallower water. I tighten into a heavy fish and the rod bends as it speeds away up the glide. Surprisingly, it halts at the top and I realise that in all probability it will seek to get me tangled in the roots of the trees that line the glide. I lift the rod and use as much pressure as I dare in the hope of lifting the fish and getting its nose up. Once I can "drown" it there will be more hope of bringing it in without a break. Surprisingly, it comes up, flounders, and I speed it along the surface to the net. It is a beauty: three and a half pounds, short for its weight and plump in the beam. I steady it, holding it in the water, where it remains for three seconds and then is away. I cross the ford and hurry down to the bottom of the reach where I fished a few hours ago.

All is quiet in the early evening. Amazing. I can see one or two rises already, and I lose no time in wading to the middle and aiming at something which seems to be shouldering the water. The fly is taken and the fish landed and returned – another three-quarter-pounder. On to the next and the next with the same result. I am beginning to lose count. Surely this is an unusual bonanza for this stretch. The sun is leaving the water but the air is still warm...surprisingly so for late summer. These have been windless, balmy days of limpid mornings and afternoons of murmurous calm. I move on to the top of the reach just below the place where the ford provides a shallower crossing. Here the water is deeper, the surface less cobbled with rounded wavelets. A fish is rising regularly just below the crossing, where there seems to be a small shelf. Here is where the level of the riverbed seems to fall about a foot or so. The surface is smooth, and I use a little more care here as I cast to the rise. The take is instant and I am soon bringing a lusty fish to the net – a pound and a half. This must be the last of the day. I leave the water and cross the ford back to the car. Upstream, under the trees where I took my best fish of the day, I can see a quiver on the liquid darkness of the surface, then another. Something is sipping there, just too far up under the tangle of the trees for me to reach. Another big fish having a late supper? Hey ho! I watch for a few minutes as the dusk gathers, then I doff my waders, break my rod, light a cigarette, and am on my way back through the late evening to the cottage and my own supper.

The days have slipped by with alarming speed and a multiplicity of new experiences. Sadly, "the fairest things have fleetest end." I now know every angle and corner of the reach where I fished on my first day here. I have even fished the lakes in spare moments at noon, and seen the evening draw its "gradual, dusky veil" over Egdon Heath after the finality of the end of the evening rise. I have walked back to the cottage at dusk with glow-worms lending a magic to my steps. I have hung over bridges by thatched cottages and seen everywhere the river waters purling through reeds and cresses ... trouty places all. Only step over a plank across a feeder stream and a bow-wave indicates that even here some trout has found a feeding place. Tomorrow I shall fish the Frome, a river name instinct with the mood of Hardy's novels, often imagined in my boyhood reading of his books. As I fall asleep I imagine the rain pouring down that night on the Frome, and the pool where the desperate Eustacia threw herself and was drowned.

I arrive at the Frome through a mass of willow herb hung with cobwebs and spiders' webs gleaming in the morning sunlight. At the river there is yellow and purple loosestrife, and blackberries gleam in low bushes. I sample one or two, and watch the dragonflies hovering, their wings gleaming, their bodies iridescent. The river is broader, fuller, swifter than the waters I have fished in the last few days. Downstream is a broad, graceful stone bridge. My beat is upstream from here. The water is rapid and broken, interspersed with runs of deeper water. Nothing is showing on the surface on this sunny morning, so I shall explore my three-quarters of a mile yard by yard with a sunk fly cast up and across. Nothing is more full of the promise of the unexpected than a stretch of a new river on a sunny morning such as this. I have been told by the friendly proprietor that beyond my limit is a branch stream which I have permission to fish – "infinite riches in a little space!" I tie on a sparsely hackled Greenwell's Glory (the "G.G." of so many victories in past days) and throw it into the current just ahead and across, not wishing to spoil the nearer water where there may be fish. A few casts produce no results, then as I lengthen the cast and quickly mend the lie to avoid drag there is a tightening, a line of fine spray as the line lifts and the rod bends. I am taken upstream and down again, and I rejoice in the absence on these chalkstreams of any of those snags, fallen branches, submerged tree-trunks, even barbed wire, so often encountered on others waters. Another blessing is the shallowness of the riverbanks and the sense of being close to the level of the water. I manage to raise his nose and bring him on his side to the net, a two-pounder of spectacular power and beauty. I return him to the water and he is off in a flash, none the worse for the encounter. There is, for me at least, immense satisfaction in returning a trout unharmed.

For the next two hours I am rewarded by several captures and one or two "takes". Nothing has risen, or perhaps, because of the boisterous current, I have seen nothing rise. I take a short break and drink a cup of the hot coffee I have for once remembered to bring in the thermos. The midday sun is filling the meadows around me with a warm, mellow light. One or two bees are sending their soporific buzzings to mingle with the more insistent, more assertive sounds of the river. Beyond me is a sharp bend and a sort of bottleneck where the river narrows into a short strait before opening out again. There the current is fast, and a fall in the river level gives it added speed. I approach and ponder. I remove the G.G. and tie on a large, heavily weighted nymph. I throw it upstream a few yards, let it sink, and ease it without drag into the narrows and down beyond. To my great surprise it is taken, and the rod bends double as the line is taken out at speed. I move quickly downstream, keeping the rod well bent, glad to know he is now well clear of the turbulent torrent where he seized my mayfly nymph. Here the river is broader, and so far as I can see, there are no great hazards in the now slower, more even current. But I have a nagging doubt as I play this lively fish and I realise that a longshank weighted nymph has been tied to a three-pound leader, and this "craves wary walking". I steer, release line, wind in when the tension slackens, and cringe when he shoots away with a scream of the reel, then pauses, head wagging viciously to and fro in an effort to free himself of this unexpected restraint. I have spotted a small inlet of calm water further down, and it is here that I hope to guide him to the net. A few more spurts in various directions and I manage to get his nose up, then a rapid pull has him flat on his side so that he comes to the net easily, to my surprise and relief. I hang the net on the spring scale, deduct the weight of the net, and the result is three and a half pounds. As I place him back in the water he takes three seconds to recover and is off.

Two or three light balloons of winged seed drift across the stream and once more my ears respond to the rush and gurgle of the water. I light a cigarette and squat on the bank A few waterboatmen jerk to and fro in the miniature world round my waders and a bee, heavy with pollen, oars its way up into the air and away. The somniferous spell of August hangs heavy all around me, and as if in conspiracy, the sounds, the scents, the mellow hues of flowers, weeds and cresses lay their powerful enchantments on me, and Morpheus takes me off, volens nolens, to his House of Sleep.

How long have I been here, my feet in the water, flat on my back? I rouse as if I had been drugged, surprised to find my rod beside me, and nothing changed in the scene around me. My watch tells me I have been asleep for almost an hour. Here there are no hints of the world of human beings, and for a moment I feel somehow cut off from the friendly hum of men. Obviously those long winters alone which Thoreau spent by Walden Pond are not for me, nor those arctic winters which certain self-sufficient stalwarts spent alone in the cause of their scientific researches. Give me any day the music of humanity, however still or sad, in preference to living in paradise alone. But enough of these drowsy musings! We are fishing the Dorset Frome on a sunny day in August, and that should be enough to satisfy even the most introspective of souls.

I walk upstream to the little tributary which the proprietor recommended. It differs from the main stream. It cuts its way through borders of sedges, running calm and clear for three or four hundred yards of very tempting, fishable water. I wade across to the right bank and survey the scene. The lowering sun has thrown most of the stream into shadow, and this should help. As I gaze, I spot a rise, and one or two tremblings on the surface further upstream. Off comes the Mayfly nymph and I attach my Grey Duster with its parachute tying. This should facilitate light landings on this smooth surface. I am more than surprised to see fish rising and silently thank the proprietor for pointing me in this direction. I kneel down and edge forward. The fish rises again, conveniently in midstream. The fly sails out and lands as light as thistledown a yard short. I let it drift back for four or five yards and cast again. It kisses the water, well cocked, and trembles back a foot, two feet, and is taken. I tighten and strain the rod as much as I dare, hoping to play the fish without spoiling the water further upstream. I soon have his nose up, and he comes to the net, a lovely spotted leopard of just over a pound. I return him and dry the fly with some powder I carry for the purpose.

I anchor the fly in the rod butt and pause for a moment. I become aware of the more subtle sounds wandering into the consciousness from this offshoot of the river. There are low-pitched gurgles, brief pauses, then slightly stronger surges, then almost silence; then the sequence begins again "with tremulous cadence low". It is a music of haunting beauty, like moments in a Schubert impromptu. I almost forget what I am about as I surrender to these delicious cadences. The air is still warm, but the heat of the afternoon has given way to the coolness of early evening, and something tells me that it is time for me to say goodbye to this enchanting place, in spite of the possibilities it is still promising. I gaze upstream as the sound of a rising fish startles the quiet where I stand. I watch the lusty rings as they disperse, swaying the reeds on either side. Let it feed in peace, I say to myself, and before I can fall into temptation, I break the rod, detach the fly, and wade across through the swell of the stream to the other side. This is my last day I remind myself as I cross the meadow where the day's insect life is now silent, and stow my kit in the car.

Later, washed and fed, I wander out for a last evening gaze over Egdon Heath. It has been one of those weeks of warm days, and evenings of almost haunting calm, a harvest moon casting a glow over a spellbound landscape. The Piddle and the Frome, out there, still running clear and sure through their reeds and cresses, have them now to themselves, as they have been for centuries of such evenings. I bid them farewell, and hear their music in my sleep, as I hear it again as I write – "the spirit ditties of no tone". Who knows if I shall come here again? Better, perhaps, not to break the spell.

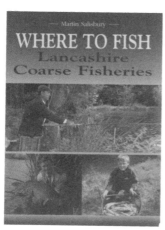

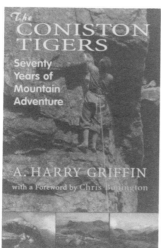

Also from Sigma Leisure:

WHERE TO FISH: LANCASHIRE COARSE FISHERIES
Martin Salisbury
Endorsed by Martin James, presenter of BBC Radio Lancashire's "From the Water's Edge", this is the definitive guide to angling in Lancashire - from places on your doorstep to those you've never heard of! The book covers 113 fisheries - including stillwaters, rivers and canals, and includes details of species, rules, tickets, costs and access for each fishery. Nearby amenities are also featured to make your day complete. £6.95

STILLWATER TROUT FISHING IN NE ENGLAND
Bob Smith & Alan Young
This is the only book that provides detailed information for anglers in the North-East. Location maps, details of fisheries, recommended flies and tackle shops are all listed. Both private stillwaters and those owned by Northumbrian Water are included. A detailed trout fishing log and high-quality photographs complement the invaluable information. £7.95

THE CONISTON TIGERS: Seventy Years of Mountain Adventure
A. Harry Griffin
This is the story of A. Harry Griffin MBE, Country Diary writer for *The Guardian*. "A living history of modern Lakeland climbing" - Chris Bonington. "The book which thousands have been willing Harry to write." - Alan Rusbridger, Editor of *The Guardian*. "Prose tumbles off the page as clear as a mountain stream - a classic of mountain literature" - Bill Birkett, mountain writer & photographer. "... one of the great outdoor writers of the century." - Cameron McNeish, Editor of *The Great Outdoors*. £9.95 (paperback edition)

All of our books are available through booksellers. In case of difficulty, or for a free catalogue, please contact: SIGMA LEISURE,
1 SOUTH OAK LANE, WILMSLOW, CHESHIRE SK9 6AR.
Phone: 01625-531035   Fax: 01625-536800.
E-mail: info@sigmapress.co.uk
Web site: http//www.sigmapress.co.uk
MASTERCARD and VISA orders welcome.